Poem
of the Cid

Poem
of the Cid

A modern translation with

notes by Paul Blackburn

Edited and with a Foreword

by George Economou

Introduction by Luis Cortest

University of Oklahoma Press : Norman

This translation is dedicated to Jean Séguy and René Nelli
in Toulouse and Carcassonne, respectively,
and to Robert Creeley, my first publisher,
who managed to get me to Spain in the first place.

Excerpt from "January Morning," by William Carlos Williams, is from *The Collected Poems of William Carlos Williams, Volume I: 1909–1939*, copyright © 1938, 1991, New Directions Publishing Corporation. Reprinted by permission of New Directions.

Library of Congress Cataloging-in-Publication Data

Cantar de mío Cid. English
   Poem of the Cid : a modern translation with notes by Paul Blackburn / edited with a foreword by George Economou ; introduction by Luis Cortest.
     p.   cm.
   Includes bibliographical references.
   ISBN 0-8061-3021-0 (cloth : alk. paper). — ISBN 0-8061-3022-9 (paper)
   I. Blackburn, Paul.   II. Economou, George.   III. Cid (Epic cycle)   IV. Title.
PQ6367.E3B513   1998
861' . 1—dc21   97-43704
                                          CIP

Text design by Alicia Hembekides. Typeface is Trump Medieval.

The paper in this book meets the guidelines for permanence and durability of the Committee on Production Guidelines for Book Longevity of the Council on Library Resources, Inc. ∞

A translation of *Poema de Mío Cid* copyright © 1966 by Paul Blackburn and American R. D. M. Corporation. Copyright assigned to Joan Blackburn in 1972 and transferred to the University of Oklahoma Press in 1996. New edition copyright © 1998 by the University of Oklahoma Press, Norman, Publishing Division of the University. All rights reserved. Manufactured in the U.S.A.

1 2 3 4 5 6 7 8 9 10

Contents

Translator's Preface, by Paul Blackburn   VII

Foreword, by George Economou   IX

Introduction, by Luis Cortest   XI

THE FIRST CANTAR

    The Cid's Exile   3

THE SECOND CANTAR

    The Wedding of the Cid's Daughters   59

THE THIRD CANTAR

    The Atrocity at Corpes   111

Notes   169

Selected References   175

Translator's Preface

By Paul Blackburn

The first thing to know about this translation is that it is reasonably literal, and that departures from this reasonable standard are in the interest of equivalent weights in modern American English. The second point is that it is made specifically to be read aloud. The student reading it to himself should take this seriously. Rather than reading it separately, students studying the poem might choose the best reader among them to listen to or might alternate reading sections to one another.

The original was made to be sung or chanted in the presence of an audience by the *juglar*, the professional musician, in the context of a court. To try to bring across this aspect of a medieval epic seems to me more important to our sense of the work than to try to approximate line length, caesura, and the steadily recurring assonances. This was attempted successfully by my contemporary William S. Merwin, whose introduction to the poem in the Modern Library edition is especially valuable. I am also indebted to him specifically for the lovely formulation (II, 95) of don Jerónimo's epithet, "the mitred man of merit," which I could not resist stealing. Anyone particularly interested in a version stressing the poetics of the work should read his version also.

A heavier debt, and a completely unreturnable one, I owe to the great Spanish philologist Ramón Menéndez

Pidal, who worked on this fine poem literally all his life (see Selected References). His edition of the poem, with its historical introduction and detailed notes, as well as his other books on the Cid and on poetry of medieval Spain, have been invaluable to me.

I wish also to thank John Mong, who first suggested that I undertake the translation; Professor Glen Willbern, the editor of the Study Master series, whose encouragement and suggestions have lifted, curbed, and sustained me; and not least, my wife, Sara, whose support, encouragement, and good cheer throughout have made it truly possible to complete such a cranky project. Please enjoy it, and remember, read it aloud.

Foreword

By George Economou

When I visited with my friend Paul Blackburn for the last time in August 1971, just a few weeks before his death on September 13, neither of us fully understood the consequences of the personal contract we made with each other on that sad, sunny afternoon in upstate New York. Our only immediate literary concern that day was our agreement that I would prepare his collection of translations of the troubadours for publication. Little did we know that the commitment to find a publisher for *Proensa* (University of California Press, 1978) would be transformed into another, unexpected and unarticulated commitment that would last the next quarter of the century. With the placement of a few translations of Apollonaire in an anthology and the publication of *Lorca/Blackburn* (Momo's Press, 1979), the blank space of "unpublished translations" had been filled. Or so it seemed. Then around 1980, I learned that the American R. D. M. Corporation, which had published Blackburn's translation of the Spanish epic *Poema de Mío Cid* under its Study Master imprint in 1966, had gone out of existence, taking with it what I and many others recognized as the finest English translation of a great medieval poem.

It was apparent not only to me but to many poets, readers, teachers, and Hispanists as well that Paul Blackburn's *Poem of the Cid* had to be rescued from the limbo of out-of-print books. A text out of circulation and barely extant in a scattering of rare copies, the translation's legendary reputation has continued to grow. Numerous friends have urged me over the years to find a way to reprint or republish it. Unnecessary but much appreciated, that urging and support have sustained me in my effort to bring about a rebirth of this splendid work of literary translation. Many publishers showed genuine interest, but conditions were never quite right to result in a second incarnation. Finally, with the help of editors John Drayton and Kimberly Wiar of the University of Oklahoma Press, the *Poem of the Cid* now appears in a new edition with a new introduction, updated bibliography, and textual corrections and restorations of several words to the translator's original version.

In his lifetime, Paul Blackburn learned much about the difficulties and triumphs of translation. When all was said and done, he claimed, "Much depends upon the translator (also upon the reader)." His words are reminiscent of the bond between poet and reader expressed in William Carlos Williams's "January Morning" (xv):

> I wanted to write a poem
> that you would understand.
> For what good is it to me
> if you can't understand it?
> But you got to try hard—

Blackburn's conviction argues for the primacy of that unity of the arts of writing and of reading. With this new edition of the *Poem of the Cid*, a special bond between translator and reader has been restored.

Introduction

By Luis Cortest

Few works in the history of medieval Western literature have had the national impact that the *Poema de Mío Cid* (*Poem of the Cid*) has had on Spanish literary tradition. Based on the life of the eleventh-century military commander Rodrigo Díaz de Vivar (c. 1043–99), the poem describes a series of events surrounding the exile of the protagonist, called the Cid. The *Poem of the Cid* is the only example of medieval Spanish epic that survives virtually intact; only a few fragments remain from other works of this genre. The value of this poem is even greater because only one manuscript of the text exists. In spite of the lack of diffusion suggested by the survival of only one manuscript, a vast literary tradition has emerged from the poem. The figure of the Cid (from the Arabic *Sayyidī* or "My Lord") was celebrated in the Spanish popular ballad tradition for hundreds of years after this epic poem was composed. It is estimated that over two hundred such ballads survive.

The *Poem of the Cid* is important for literary reasons, but it is also important for historical reasons. The poem provides the reader with great insight into the period of medieval Spanish history that is generally called the "Reconquest": the long period in Spanish history that begins just after the time of the first Moorish incursion into the Iberian Peninsula from North Africa in 711 and ends with the conquest of Granada in 1492. Those centuries of Moorish occupation were a time of war and constant change. The movement of the Reconquest was from north to south, creating ever-changing borders as territories were reconquered by Christian armies and then, often, lost and reconquered. The Spain of the Cid could perhaps best be described as a configuration of several small kingdoms struggling to remain Christian or Moorish in a time of war or the ever-present threat of war. In that society of warriors and soldiers in which the Spanish national identity was forged, Rodrigo Díaz de Vivar was, without a doubt, the greatest and most feared of military leaders. Yet, despite his outstanding reputation, the Cid's relationship with his king, Alfonso VI, was quite problematic. Rodrigo Díaz de Vivar was exiled twice by King Alfonso VI, the first time from 1081 to 1087 and again from 1089 to 1092. At an earlier time, the Cid had been the strong supporter of King Sancho of Castille, the brother and rival of Alfonso. Sancho was killed at the siege of Zamora in 1072 by a supporter (if not a family member) of King Alfonso. The Cid, therefore, never enjoyed Alfonso's complete trust.

In the *Poem of the Cid*, Rodrigo Díaz de Vivar, the hero, is the loyal vassal, while King Alfonso appears as a man of poor judgment and cruel indignation. As the poem begins, the jealous enemies of the Cid have poisoned the mind of the king, who then responds by sending the Cid into exile. The Cid, determined to win back his honor, resolutely continues his efforts to regain his reputation. Through his own heroic efforts, by winning one military campaign after another, the Cid eventually regains all that he has lost as a result of his expulsion from Alfonso's kingdom.

Although the Cid is indeed an epic hero, he is not always seen as larger than life. In addition to being depicted as a superlative warrior, he is also portrayed as a loving husband and a caring father. Yet, when his daughters are dishonored by the cowardly Infantes de Carrión, he does not seek personal revenge. The Cid respects the laws of his society and proceeds to seek justice in an appropriate "legal" manner. The Cid is both the model of the loyal vassal and an example of courage and restraint. In the end, the Cid is rewarded for his patience and for his loyalty. It would be difficult to imagine a more perfect medieval military commander.

The modern reader may be appalled by the Cid's treatment of the Jews (Raquel and Vidas); however, it must be remembered that the age of the Cid was a time of open antisemitism. The medieval Christian audience of the poem probably found the actions of the Cid in that encounter acceptable (or perhaps even laudable). Still, in an age when war rages on between Christians and Moslems, the Cid maintains a positive relationship with some Moslem leaders characterized in the text. This literary detail is, in fact, compatible with historical record. During the Reconquest, Moors and Christians often formed alliances with one another. In his own day, the Cid was greatly admired by at least some Moorish leaders.

Curiously, despite the powerful influence of the *Poem of the Cid*, many scholarly problems remain unsolved. First among these is the unyielding and complex issue of authorship: Is there a known author of the poem? Second, is the *Poem of the Cid* the work of one author or of several? The first question is not difficult to answer, since the *Poem of the Cid*, like so many other medieval works, has no identifiable author. The second question is far more difficult to resolve, for there are two distinct schools of thought that try to address this issue. The first group, which we might call the "individualists," argues that the poem was most likely composed by one poet. This group of scholars contends that the most important evidence in the quest to determine the poem's authorship is both textual and historical. On the one hand, the fact that the text of the poem survives in only one early thirteenth-century manuscript copied by a single scribe makes discussion of the different versions of the poem somewhat problematic. On the other hand, the text of the poem, which this group of scholars views as a masterpiece of literary and artistic unity, includes references to specific historical and, in particular, legal details that would seem to indicate the poem was composed by a single author who was familiar with those matters.

The second group of scholars, which might be called the "oralists," believe that the *Poem of the Cid* grew directly out of Spanish popular tradition. The most important figure in this group was the great Spanish scholar, Ramon Menéndez Pidal, whom Paul Blackburn praises in the Translator's Preface. The oralists, or "neotraditionalists" as they are sometimes called, contend that an oral epic tradition flourished in Spain during the Middle Ages. This group contends that the poems themselves existed in many different versions, depending on the individual performer or singer (*juglar*). The oralists believe that at least two different authors contributed to the composition of the *Poem of the Cid*. The most important evidence for this theory is the language of the text. On the basis of linguistic differences, the oralists argue that different authors most likely composed different sections of the text. The oralists also contend that the language of the poem is characteristic of the twelfth rather than the early thirteenth century.

It is extremely difficult to establish a date for the text. The individualists believe the poem dates from the first years of the thirteenth century and give great importance to the date of the surviving manuscript. The oralists argue for an earlier date, maintaining that the poem was probably composed about sixty years after the death of Rodrigo Díaz de Vivar. They contend that the *Poem of the Cid* is a work of art, but that it is, nevertheless, based on historical events. Events from the life of the Cid are narrated in a Latin chronicle (*Historia Roderici*) that dates from the time of Rodrigo Díaz de Vivar.

In order to understand the basis of the debate over the date of the poem more clearly, we might consider the fact that most medieval Western vernacular epics have little connection to actual historical events. In fact, these texts are usually highly fictional creations that include many supernatural episodes. The *Poem of the Cid* is quite different in this regard. The hero of the poem, Rodrigo Díaz de Vivar, did have a wife named Ximena and two daughters who married Prince Ramiro of Navarre and Ramón Berenguer III, Count of Barcelona. It is also a matter of historical record that in June 1094, the Cid completed the conquest of Valencia. This event did take place after the Cid had been exiled by King Alfonso for the second time. Obviously, some details have been modified (for example, the true names of the daughters of the Cid were Cristina and María). However, the poem does contain quite a number of historically accurate elements.

Finally, the most fundamental question about the text has little or nothing to do with the poem's historical context: What exactly makes this poem so attractive and appealing? It may well be that the perennial appeal of the poem is its richly thematic nature. In this medieval poem we find almost all of the most important themes of Spanish literature: honor, justice, loyalty, treachery, and jealousy. These are themes that appear and reappear in the literature of Spain for centuries after their first appearance in the *Poem of the Cid*. Another attractive feature of the poem is the way in which history and fiction are fused. Historical fiction has a long history in the West, and in this particular case the events narrated were surely quite familiar to the poem's intended audience. In this sense, the poem is a model of refashioned history.

No matter what gives this poem its great appeal, the fact is that the *Poem of the Cid* left its mark on subsequent literature for centuries after the manuscript was produced. It is highly unlikely that the manuscript of the text was ever seen by the vast majority of those later poets who composed works in the Cid tradition. The Cid as a literary figure, however, survived in the ballad tradition in Spain and even had an impact on other Western literatures. For the modern reader, the fictionalized events of the Cid's life still remain a source of great interest and enjoyment.

Poem
of the Cid

THE FIRST CANTAR

The Cid's Exile

Since the first manuscript leaf of the Cantar is lost, the opening of the story (in brackets) is supplied from the Chronicle of Twenty Kings. *The Latin prose of that book had, in the first place, been abridged and translated from the vernacular of the poem itself, so that the particulars will be much the same.*

KING ALFONSO SENDS THE CID TO COLLECT THE ANNUAL RENTS FROM THE MOORISH KING OF SEVILLA. THE LATTER IS ATTACKED BY THE CASTILLIAN COUNT, GARCÍA ORDÓÑEZ. SUPPORTING THE KING OF CASTILLE'S MOORISH VASSAL, THE CID BEATS GARCÍA ORDÓÑEZ AT CABRA, CAPTURES HIM, AND INSULTS HIM. THE CID RETURNS TO CASTILLE WITH THE TRIBUTE, BUT HIS ENEMIES MAKE TROUBLE FOR HIM WITH THE KING. THE KING BANISHES THE CID.

[THE KING, don Alfonso, sent Ruy Díaz, mio Cid, for the rents due every year from the kings of Córdoba and Sevilla. Almutamiz, king of Sevilla, and Almudafar, king of Granada, were at that time bitterest enemies; their hate was a mortal hate. And with the king of Granada at that time were some noblemen who supported him: the count don García Ordóñez; the son-in-law of King García of Navarre, Fortún Sánchez; and Lope Sánchez, among others. And each of these rich men supported Almudafar,

3

king of Granada, with all his power, and these powers
were directed against Almutamiz, king of Sevilla.

The Cid Ruy Díaz, when he heard that they were
coming against Almutamiz, vassal and tributary of his
lord, King Alfonso, he took it badly and was very angry.
He sent letters of petition to all of them, asking why they
would want to march against the king of Sevilla, and
asking that they not come and destroy his lands, for they
owed allegiance to their king, don Alfonso. And should
they still insist upon it, they could hardly expect Alfonso
not to come to his vassal's aid; after all, he was his tribu-
tary. The king of Granada and those nobles paid no atten-
tion to the Cid's letters, threw themselves violently into
the campaign and destroyed the king of Sevilla's lands as
far over as the castle of Cabra.

When the Cid Ruy Díaz saw this, he mustered all the
men he could find, Christian and Moor alike, and marched
against the king of Granada to drive him from the king of
Sevilla's lands.

Almudafar and the Castillian noblemen with him,
when they heard that the Cid was on his way, sent word
that they were not going to get out of the country because
of him. And when Ruy Díaz heard this, he decided that
there was nothing for it, he would have to attack them.

And he did. He went against them in the field, and the
battle lasted from early morning until noon. Losses were
heavy on the king of Granada's side, Moors and Christians
alike, and the Cid beat them and drove them off the field.
In this battle, the Cid took García Ordóñez prisoner and
pulled out a hunk of his beard,[1] and took prisoner plenty
of other nobles, and so many other men that they kept no
count of them.

The Cid kept the prisoner for three days and then set
the whole lot of them free. While they were being so held,

he ordered his men to collect from the battlefield the belongings and riches which lay about. Then the Cid returned with all his company and the booty to Almutamiz in Sevilla, and gave him, and all the Moors, whatever of the loot they recognized as their own, and whatever they wanted to take besides.

And from that day on, Moor and Christian alike called him: Ruy Díaz de Bivar, el Cid Campeador, which is to say, The Fighter.

Almutamiz made him many fine gifts and gave him the tribute for which he had come. The Cid returned with all the tribute to king don Alfonso, his lord. The king gave him a fine welcome and showed himself highly pleased with the Cid and with whatever he'd done down there. Many were jealous of him for the king's favor, and, seeking to do him in, suggested that all the tax money had not reached the treasury, which got him into a lot of trouble with the king. Alfonso, who had an ancient grudge against him, proved only too willing to listen to the gossip and believe it. He sent the Cid word that he was exiled from the kingdom.

The Cid, when he read the letter, was heavy with grief, but did not wish to do otherwise than comply. He'd been given only nine days' grace in which to leave the country.]

The bracketed first part of this next section is translated from a reconstruction in poetry from the Chronicle; an indication is made where the manuscript itself begins.

I   THE CID CALLS HIS VASSALS TOGETHER. THEY'LL GO
INTO EXILE WITH HIM.

[He sent for his vassals and relatives
          and told them that he was under the king's
                    edict, that he be clear out of the country within nine days.
And he would like to know which of them wanted to go with him
                    and which would stay.
"And those who want to go with me, may God help you,
          and those who want to stay,
                    fine, I'll go away pleased."
                    Then his first cousin,
                         Álvar Fáñez, spoke up:
"We're with you, Cid,
no matter what, wild
territory or town,
and while we're in one piece, we'll never fail you. We'll
wear out everything around, our goods, the
horses, the mules, our clothes,
and, as your loyal vassals, serve you always."
                    Everyone shouted together, "That's
                    right!" to what don Álvaro had said.
The Cid thanked them deeply for what
had been decided there.
                         Mio Cid went out from Bivar
                         heading down to Burgos,
                              left his palaces desolate,
                              unoccupied by his own.]

          (Here, Per Abbat's manuscript begins.)

He
turned and looked back to see the towers,
                    tears running from his eyes:

saw the gates standing ajar,
doors left open without locks,
the porches bare
                          of either pelts or coverings,
perches empty of falcons, empty of molted hawks. He sighed,
mio Cid, his worries were weighty, and not small.
The Cid spoke well and with great measure:
                          "Thanks be to thee, my Lord, our
                          Father, which art in heaven!
                          It's my enemies have turned
                          this treachery upon me."

2   OMENS ON THE ROAD TO BURGOS.

Then they set spur to horse,
loosed the reins, they opened up then.
Crows flew across to their right
as they were leaving Bivar,
and as they drove down to Burgos,
crows crossed to their left.
The Cid shrugged and shook his head:
        "So, we're thrown out of the country, well,
        cheer up, Fáñez! When we come back to Castille, we'll
                come back with all the honors."

3   THE CID ENTERS BURGOS.

The Cid Ruy Díaz came into Burgos,
the pennons of sixty lances with him.
        They have to get a look at him,
        men and women both.
            Townsmen and their wives crowd the windows,
                tears in their eyes
                and in their mouths

a single sentence:
>"God, what a good vassal!
>If only he had a worthy lord."

4   NO ONE WILL PUT THE CID UP. ONLY A SMALL GIRL
ADDRESSES HIM, AND THAT TO TELL HIM TO GO AWAY. THE CID
FINDS HE HAS TO MAKE CAMP OUTSIDE OF TOWN, ON THE SAND
OF THE RIVERBANK.

They would have invited him gladly,
only not one dared,
>so great was Alfonso's fury.
>The night before, his letter,
>sealed with severity and heavy with warnings,
>had gotten to Burgos:
that
to mio Cid Ruy Díaz
no man should give shelter,
or by the king's true word, he'd lose
his goods, his eyes from his head, his soul, and his body.
>Everyone was ashamed, and in sorrow,
>hid from mio Cid,
>>and no one chanced a word.
The Campeador rode up to a place
they could stay for the night, and
when he reached the door he found it barred.
For fear of the king they had agreed
>that, unless he broke it down, by
>no means to let him in.
The Cid's men called loudly to those inside,
>they did not answer a word. Mio
>Cid dug in his spurs, raced up to the door,
pulled one foot out of the stirrup and
gave it a helluva kick.

Door was well secured and did not budge.
                          Then a little girl of nine years
                          leaned above him over the balcony:
"Hey Campeador, in a good hour you girded on sword!
          But the king has forbidden it,
          his letter arrived last night
with heavy warnings and stamped with the royal seal.
          We don't dare open to you, or
                    put you up,
                    for if we did,
                              we'd lose our goods and our houses, even
                              the eyes out of our faces. Cid,
what would you gain from our misery?
But, with all his holy strength,
may God keep you."
                          And she went back into the house.
Then the Cid saw
that he would get no privilege from the king. He
turned from the door and galloped through the town,
dismounted at the church of Santa María,
fell upon his knees
and prayed from the heart.
                          The prayer done,
                          he rode on,
                          rode out of the gates
                          and crossed the Arlanzón by the
                          bridge near the cathedral.
On the far side of the river,
on the sand of the riverbank,
he had them pitch his tent, and then dismounted.
Mio Cid Ruy Díaz,
who in good hour girded on sword, set
          his tent on the rough sand
                    surrounded by good companions,

when no one would take him in.
So the Cid set down camp
as though he were in the mountains.
In the great city of Burgos, he
was forbidden to buy anything
whatsoever, any provisions,
and no one dared sell him ration enough
to feed a single man
for a single day.

5 MARTÍN ANTOLÍNEZ COMES OUT OF TOWN WITH
PROVISIONS FOR THE CID.

Martín Antolínez, that worthy man of Burgos,
supplied the Cid and his men with wine and bread
—all of it from his own stores,
he didn't have to buy them—
so that everyone had plenty of provisions.
The worthy Campeador was pleased,
likewise, all the others with him.
Martín Antolínez spoke then,
you shall hear what he said:
"Hey Campeador,
you were born in a good hour!
Let's stay here tonight,
but let's leave first thing in the morning, for I
shall be reported for having done you a service.
King Alfonso'll
be sore as sin.
If I get away with my life and limb and join you,
sooner or later, the king
'll love me like a friend:
if not, well, I couldn't give a fig
for what I leave behind."

6   THE CID, WITHOUT RESOURCES, APPEALS TO THE
ASTUTENESS OF MARTÍN ANTOLÍNEZ.

Mio Cid spoke,
who in good hour
girded on sword:
                    "You're a stout lance, Martín Antolínez!
            And if I live, I'll see your pay is doubled.
Gold and silver, I've spent it all, and you can see
I carry nothing with me, and
I'll need something for all my men.
            Since there's no one will supply me freely,
            I'll get it by force if necessary.
Look, I've got an idea, see if you like it:
I'll have a pair of chests built, fill them with
sand, so that they're good and heavy,
stud them with great nails,
and cover them with beautifully tooled leather.

7   THE COFFERS ARE INTENDED TO GET MONEY FROM
TWO BURGOS JEWS.

"Let the leather be vermillion and the nails gilded.
            Go to Raquel and Vidas quickly
            and say to them for me:
'Since I can buy nothing in Burgos
and the king's anger pursues me,
this treasure of mine is too heavy to take with me,
and I want to pawn it for whatever is reasonable.
They should come to get it at night so that the
Christians don't see.'
            Let the Lord and all his saints besides
            witness I do this unwillingly, there's
                nothing else I can do."

8   MARTÍN ANTOLÍNEZ GOES BACK TO BURGOS TO LOOK
FOR THE JEWS.

Martín Antolínez didn't wait,
he went into Burgos by the gate,
went straight to the castle, though it was late,
and asked for Raquel and Vidas.

9   THE DEAL BETWEEN MARTÍN ANTOLÍNEZ AND THE
JEWS. THEY GO TO THE CID'S TENT. THEY CARRY AWAY THE
TRUNKS OF SAND.

> Raquel and Vidas were together counting over
> what they had earned in profits.
> Antolínez came in, all shrewdness.

"Raquel and Vidas, are you there, dear friends?
I want to speak to both of you privately."

> No waiting, all three went together
> into the back room.

"Raquel and Vidas,
both of you give me your hands, swear
you will not discover it, or me, to either Christian or Moor,
you'll lack for nothing, I'll make you rich forever.
The Campeador went to collect tribute, and
when he saw anything worth the trouble, he
kept it for himself.

> He has been accused
>   and so has come to this.
>   He has two trunks full of mint gold.

You'll understand, then, why the king is angry with him.
He's left houses and palaces, all his inheritance, and these chests
he cannot take with him, someone would sniff them out.

> The Campeador will leave them in your hands, and
> you lend him in cash whatever is reasonable.

Take the chests and keep them safe, but both of you must
swear mightily and keep your promises, not
to look into the chests for the rest of this year."
                Raquel and Vidas
                conferred together:
       "One has to get something on every piece of business,
       and of course we know he took something when
       he went into Moorish lands, he got plenty,
and a man who carries money on him doesn't sleep easy.
We'll take both trunks and hide them
where no one will sniff them out.
            But tell us how much the Cid wants,
                how much
            interest will he give us for the whole year?"
           Martín Antolínez answered and was sharp:
"Mio Cid will want
only what is reasonable, ask little of you, and leave
his treasure in your safekeeping. Needy men
are gathering to join him from everywhere,
           six hundred marks are needed."
      "We are happy to give them to him."
"Look, it's getting dark, the Cid is under pressure,
let's have the marks right away."
       "Whoa," said Raquel and Vidas, "you
       don't do business that way.
       You do the getting first, and then the giving."
"Good enough," said Antolínez, "come,
let's go together to the Campeador,
            and we'll help you,
            as is only right, to
load the trunks up, bring them across, and put them somewhere safe
where no one will ever know, Christian or Moor."
       "A deal," said Raquel and Vidas. "When the trunks are here
       you'll get the six hundred marks."

Martín Antolínez rode off quietly, Raquel
and Vidas came along willingly.
He did not take the bridge, instead, crossed by the stream so that
no one in the town of Burgos
would get wind of it.
They reach the tent
of the famous Campeador, enter,
and kiss the Cid's hands.
Mio Cid grinned and spoke to them:
"Hey, Raquel and Vidas, had you forgotten me?
You know I'm leaving the country, disinherited,
because the king is angry with me. It
looks like you'll be keeping something of mine,
and, so long as you live, you'll never be poor."
Raquel and Vidas kissed the Cid's hands.
Martín Antolínez closed the deal: that
they would lend six hundred marks against those chests
and guard them closely till the end of the year;
and to this they gave their promise, and to this swore, that
if they broke their word and opened them before,
mio Cid should not have to give them
a damn cent of interest.
Then, Martín Antolínez:
"Load the trunks up right away,
take them, Raquel and Vidas, and put them somewhere safe.
I'll go with you and bring back the marks, for
mio Cid has to be on the road
tomorrow, before cockcrow."
Loading up the chests—you could see how much they enjoyed it.
They couldn't hoist them up on the mules' backs,
though both were stalwart men.
They were merry, Raquel and Vidas,
with such a mint.
Neither one,

as long as they lived,
would ever be poor again.

10   THE CID AND THE JEWS TAKE LEAVE OF ONE ANOTHER.
MARTÍN ANTOLÍNEZ GOES BACK TO BURGOS WITH THEM.

Raquel kissed the Cid's hand: "Hey Campeador!
You girded on sword in a good hour!
You're leaving Castille and going out among strangers,
well, that's your luck, and your profits are large. Cid,
I kiss your hand,
I beg you, let me have a leather Moorish robe,
scarlet and highly prized."
"My pleasure," said the Cid, "from this moment
it's on the order books. And if I'm lucky, I'll
bring it back from there, and if not,
well, count it against the coffers."
Raquel and Vidas carted off the chests.
Martín Antolínez went back to Burgos with them,
arrived at their place discreetly.
In the palace's center
they laid down a prayer rug, and over that
a pure, white sheet, finer than any linen. On
the first throw were three hundred silver marks, don
Martín only counted them, didn't
bother to weigh them; the
other three hundred they
paid him in gold.
Antolínez had five squires with him
and loaded all of them up.
When the whole thing was done,
now listen to what he said:
"Don Raquel and don Vidas,
the chests are yours. And I,
who managed to get them for you,

well, the
baby wants a new pair of britches."

II   THE CID, PROVIDED WITH CASH BY MARTÍN
ANTOLÍNEZ, PREPARES TO MARCH.

Raquel and Vidas
drew aside for a moment:
"Let's give him a nice gift,
he found this piece of business for us, after all.
           Martín Antolínez, you're an honored man in Burgos,
           we want to make you a fine gift,
           and you have deserved it fully.
               Have yourself some britches made,
               a rich cloak of leather, and
               a fine robe besides.
As a gift we give you thirty marks, you
deserve it, and it's only just.
And you
are our witness
in the deal we've just concluded."
                   Don Martín thanked them and took the money,
                   and said good-bye to them both.
                   He was glad to get out of the house.
                   He left Burgos, crossed the Arlanzón,
                   and came to that man's tent who
                   was in good hour born.
The Cid received him,
       both arms wide:
                   "You're here, Martín Antolínez!
                   May I see the day, my faithful vassal, when
                   I can give you something!"
"Campeador, I come
with very good news indeed:
I got you six hundred marks

and thirty more for me.
Just give the order to strike camp
and we'll pull out of here fast.
We'll hear the rooster crow in San Pedro de Cardeña;
see your noble wife, cut the stay short, and get out of the kingdom
—we've got to—
                    the last day of grace is too close."

12   THE CID MOUNTS HIS HORSE AND TAKES LEAVE OF THE
CATHEDRAL OF BURGOS, PROMISING ONE THOUSAND MASSES AT
THE VIRGIN'S ALTAR.

                    These words said,
                    the tents struck,
mio Cid and his men rode off swiftly. He
turned his horse's head toward Santa María, lifted
his right hand, and crossed himself:
                    "To you, I give thanks, O God,
                    who rule heaven and earth;
grant me your favors, holy Mother of God!
As the king is angry with me, now I quit Castille,
and do not know if I shall enter again in all my days.
Defend me with your grace, Mother of glory, as I go,
and night and day stand by me and sustain me;
                    grant me this,
                    and if my luck stays with me,
fine and costly gifts I shall lay at your altar and
promise a thousand masses to be sung there."

13   MARTÍN ANTOLÍNEZ RETURNS TO THE CITY.

The great man made his farewell
willingly, and from the heart.
                         They loosen the reins
                         and set spur and go.

That loyal man of Burgos, Martín Antolínez, said:
"I'll go see my wife
who is all my cheer,
and leave instructions
for whatever has to be done.
If the king wants to take it all,
let him, I don't care. And I'll
be back with you before sunup."

14   THE CID GOES TO CARDEÑA TO SAY GOOD-BYE TO HIS
FAMILY.

> Don Martín turned back toward Burgos,
>   and the Cid spurred on
heading for San Pedro de Cardeña as
hard as he could ride; along
with those companion knights who served him well. Soon
the cocks crow, and the first signals of day
are coming when
the Campeador arrived at the abbey, and
that good man of God, abbot don Sancho, was saying matins
as day broke.
>   And doña Jimena was there with five worthy ladies
>   praying St. Peter and the Creator:
>   "You, who guide all men, protect
>   mio Cid Campeador."

15   THE MONKS OF CARDEÑA WELCOME THE CID. JIMENA
AND HER DAUGHTERS COME BEFORE THE EXILE.

> They knocked at the door and the message was carried back.
The abbot don Sancho, God! how happy he was! Everyone
with torches and candles raced across the courtyard
to welcome him who was in good hour born,
>   a jubilant welcome!

"Thanks be to God, Cid," don Sancho said, "I
see you here. The hospitality
of this house is yours."
"My thanks, worthy abbot," the Cid replied, "I
am pleased with your kindness.
I shall take a meal for myself and for my vassals.
I'm leaving the country, so I want to give you
fifty marks, and if I live,
I'll see the sum is doubled. I
don't want to cost the monastery a penny, so here,
take these hundred marks. They should keep
doña Jimena, her daughters, and her ladies for the year.
I leave you my two daughters,
keep them safe, don Sancho,
both of them and my wife,
care for all of them well,
I commend them to you.
And if the money runs out, or you need anything, still
lay it out, I'll pay you four for one."
The abbot cheerfully agreed to the terms.
Doña Jimena is coming out with her daughters,
ladies-in-waiting carry the girls in their arms.
Down on both knees she fell before the Campeador,
tears in her eyes as she kissed his hands:
"Forced out of the country by those
cheap, backbiting, lying, foulmouthed meddlers,
O Campeador!

16   JIMENA LAMENTS THE HELPLESS STATE IN WHICH THE
GIRLS WILL BE LEFT. THE CID HOPES TO MARRY THEM OFF
HONORABLY.

"Hear me, O Cid of the perfect beard, I am here
before you, I and your daughters, and they just babies,
and these ladies who wait on me. I see

that you're on your way, and that we
must be separated. For the love of Mary,
tell us what we're to do!"
                    The soft-bearded man stretched out his hands,
                    took his daughters into his arms, hugged
                    them to his chest, for he loved them well,
                    heaved a sigh and wept:
          "My perfect wife, O doña Jimena, I
          love you better than I love my soul
          and we must part in this life, you
          shall stay here and I go. If it
          please God and St. Mary, let me see the day
when I may give both
my daughters in marriage,
may luck attend me and the days be few
till I can serve you again, my honored wife!"

17   A HUNDRED CASTILLIANS GATHER IN BURGOS TO JOIN
THE CID.

The bells of San Pedro clanged out loudly, pealed and
a great feast was laid for the Campeador.
          The news of the banishment of
               mio Cid Campeador spread
                    throughout Castille. Some
men leave houses, others their lands and castles. At
the bridge over the Arlanzón, that very day there gathered
one hundred fifteen knights, all asking for the Campeador.
Martín Antolínez joined them, and
          they all headed for San Pedro
                    to meet the man who was in good hour born.

18   THE HUNDRED KNIGHTS ARRIVE AT CARDEÑA AND ARE
SWORN IN AS THE CID'S VASSALS. HE MAKES READY FOR THE ROAD
THE FOLLOWING MORNING. MATINS AT CARDEÑA. JIMENA'S

PRAYER. THE CID TAKES LEAVE OF HIS FAMILY. FINAL INSTRUC-
TIONS TO THE ABBOT OF CARDEÑA. THE CID SETS OUT ON HIS
EXILE; BY NIGHTFALL HE HAS CROSSED THE DUERO.

When mio Cid de Bivar got word
            that his forces were growing, that
                    these men thought it worth their while, he
mounted quickly and rode out to meet them.
When he came in sight of them, he broke into a wide grin.
All came up to him, and each one kissed his hand,
            to acknowledge that he was his vassal.[2] Then
                    mio Cid addressed them with feeling:
                    "I pray God
                    that before I die
                    I may be some good to you,
who've left homes and estates behind, and for my sake.
                    What you have lost,
            I'll see you regain it twice."
      Mio Cid was cheered to see his band increase, and
all these other men were pleased to be there with him.
            Six of the days of grace have gone,
three days to go, and
                    after that, not one.
The king ordered a close watch kept on the Cid, for
            when the period of grace was done,
            if he were caught within the frontier,
he wouldn't be able to buy his way out for gold or silver.
The light was fading and evening fell;
he called his knights to gather round:
                    "Now, gentlemen, listen, and let's see you smile.
                    Whatever little I have, you have your portion.
                    Now hear this, these are the orders:
                    tomorrow morning at cockcrow, saddle up.
The good abbot in San Pedro will ring us in to matins

and say the Mass of the Holy Trinity for us;
            and when that's done,
        we'll swing into the saddle and be off, for
        our time is nearly up, and there's a long ride ahead of us."
        What the Cid ordered was what they had to do.
                The night passes and the dawn is coming;
            at second cockcrow, they start getting their horses ready.
        The Cid and his wife arrive at the church, and Jimena
fell on her knees
on the steps
before the altar to pray with all her soul that God
keep Cid Campeador from harm:
                "Glorious Lord, Father
which art in heaven, who made heaven and earth
            and on the third day the seas, who
made the moon and the stars and the sun to warm us, who
within St. Mary, your mother, became flesh, born in
Bethlehem, shepherds adored and praised, three kings
        of Arabia came, adored,
            Caspar, Balthasar, and Melchior, offering
                heartfelt gifts, gold, frankincense, and myrrh.
                    You saved Jonah when he fell into the sea,
                you saved Daniel from his lions in that terrible prison,
            you saved St. Susannah from false witness, and
        San Sebastian in Rome; you
    walked upon the earth for thirty-two years, Lord, working
wonders of which we still must talk.
Wine you made out of water,
bread from stones,
brought Lazarus back to life by your holy will. You
let the Jews seize you.
In a place they call Golgotha on Mount Calvary, they
        set you on a cross, and on
            one side of you, and on the other, two

thieves, one is in paradise, the other not.
From the cross, even, you worked miracles: Longinus,
    blind all his life, thrust his spear into your side, and
        the blood ran down the shaft and anointed his hands, which,
            when he raised them to his face, he had the power of sight,
looked all about and believed in you from that hour, and so was saved.
You arose from the tomb, descended into hell of your own choice,
you burst its doors and led forth the saintly fathers.
    King of kings you are, and Father of all the world, I
      adore you and believe in you with all my will, I
        beg St. Peter that he aid my prayers for
          mio Cid el Campeador, may
            God keep him from harm.
            Though we part today,
            may we join again in this life."
The prayer done,
the mass over,
they left the church.
Everyone's ready to ride.
El Cid went and held doña Jimena; she kissed his hand, she
wept, and didn't know what to do. He
turned and looked at his daughters.
    "To God the heavenly Father, I commend you,
    now we'll part, God
    knows
    when we'll see one another again."
      He stood there weeping,
      his eyes like faucets, you've
      never seen such tears, their parting
      like the nail torn from the finger.
The company was under way, but mio Cid
still delayed them all, turning his head,
    swinging his horse about.
Minaya Álvar Fáñez spoke, and very wisely:
"Where are your strengths, Cid?

Your mother bore you in a good hour, now let's
stop fooling around and think
   about getting this thing moving. Look,
   even all this pain will turn to joy at last.
God gave us our souls, he'll give us guidance, too."
    Still he turned, and again
   he charged the abbot to
care well for doña Jimena, for the two girls, for
the ladies who served them; once more
the abbot don Sancho was promised rich recompense.
Don Sancho turned to Álvar Fáñez who spoke:
    "If you see any men coming this way, abbot, who want to
    join us, tell them to pick up our trail and ride hard: they'll
    catch up with us, if not in open country, then in some town."
They let out rein and gallop off finally, for
the time draws near when they have to be clear of the kingdom.
The Cid got to Espinazo de Can by
bedtime, and that night men came
from everywhere to join him.
Next morning they rode out.
The loyal Campeador is quitting the land,
   keeping to the left of San Esteban, a fine city, and
    through Alcubilla at the edge of Castille.
They reached the Quinea highroad, and crossed it,
and at Navapalos the river Duero, and crossed it,
made camp for the night at Figuerela.
    Men kept coming in
    from all sides,
     to join him.

19 THE LAST NIGHT THE CID SLEEPS IN CASTILLE. AN
ANGEL COMFORTS THE EXILE.

     After nightfall, mio Cid lay down there, and
     slept so deeply that a sweet dream came over him,

                          the angel Gabriel came to him in a vision:
"Ride on, good Campeador, for never
has any man ridden forth at a better
moment, all that's yours will prosper
as long as you shall live."

                          When the Cid woke, he crossed himself.

20   THE CID CAMPS ON THE BORDER OF CASTILLE.

He crossed himself, commended himself to God,
very cheered up because of the dream he'd had.
They take to horse the next morning,
for this is the last day of stipulated time. Know that
no more time is left.

                    At the Sierra de Miedes,
                      the day's ride halted;
to their left, the towers
of Atienza, held by the Moors.

21   THE RECKONING OF THE CID'S TROOPS.

Not sundown yet, there was still some daylight.
The Cid ordered his troops into formation
              for roll call. Not
              counting the foot,
and brave men they were, he counted
three hundred lances, and on each one a pennant.

22   THE CID PUSHES ON INTO THE MOORISH KINGDOM OF
TOLEDO, A TRIBUTARY OF KING ALFONSO.

          "Feed the horses early, and God help you! Anyone
          who wants to take time to eat now, fine; and those
          who don't, well, we're riding. We're

going to cross the sierra, and that's rough and high, but
we can leave Alfonso's territory tonight.
Anyone looking for us can find us later."
They cross the range by night, morning is come and they
are starting down the ridge on the far side.
In the middle of a great marvelous wood, the Cid halted
so that the horses could be fed. He
told them he wanted to ride all night again. Good
vassals that they were, and had spirit, what-
       ever their lord commanded, they were ready.
          Before night fell again, they were off and riding.
Mio Cid traveled all night so that no one might
discover their movements. And all night, they pushed it without a rest.
Above the river Henares, at a place called Castejón,
         mio Cid and all his troops
           lay in concealment.

23   BATTLE PLANS. CASTEJÓN FALLS TO THE CID'S POWER BY
SURPRISE. A FORAGING PARTY GOES AGAINST ALCALÁ.

All night the Cid lay in concealment, as
Álvar Fáñez Minaya
advised:
      "Ya Cid, you girded on sword in a good hour!
      When we've taken it by ambush
      you stay here in Castejón and cover us from the rear,
      keep here
          one hundred of the company. Give me
        two hundred as a raiding party and with God's help and your good luck
          we'll make a good-sized profit."
"Now you're talking, Minaya," said the Campeador.
"Take the two hundred for the raid, and take
Álvar Salvadórez, no fault with him, and Álvar Álvarez,
and Galindo García, that mighty lance, all good knights,

let them go with Minaya.
And strike boldly, leave no plunder behind for fear.
Take your raiders down to Hita, through Guadalajara,
                as far as Alcalá,
and let them take all the booty they can,
leave nothing behind; don't be afraid of the Moors. I'll
keep a hundred men here and stay behind to hold
                Castejón, it'll
        serve very well as our base of operations.
        If anything happens to you on the raid, send
        word back to me to the rear at once—
                all of Spain will talk of the way
                I come to your aid."
They call out the names of those to go on the raid,
and the names of those who will stay with the
Cid at the base of operations in the rear.
The first light of dawn, morning coming, the
                sun rose, God! how handsome it was!
        Everyone getting up in Castejón,
                opening their doors, going
                        out to work in the fields,
                                to see to their lands and terraces.
                Now all are outside the walls,
        leaving the gates open.
        Only a few are left in Castejón, and
those without the gates are dispersed,
each to his own.
The Campeador sailed out of the ambush,
        surrounded the town. They
                seized the Moors and their women
                        and whatever herds there were about.
                Mio Cid don Rodrigo swept
                up to the gate.
                        The guards there,

                filled with terror
           by the swiftness of the assault,
             fled their posts, the
          gate was left unguarded.
Mio Cid Ruy Díaz rode in at the gate, a naked sword in his hand.
Fifteen Moors who got in his way he slew. He had
taken Castejón with its gold and silver. His
knights begin to come in with the plunder.
All this they count as little,
        give it all to mio Cid.
                Now, let's see
                the 203
                in the raiding party downriver.
           Without hesitation they ride
           sacking the whole countryside.
Minaya's standard went down as far as Alcalá, and from there
back up the Henares, through Guadalajara, returning with the loot.
Great piles of plunder with them, herds
        of cattle, flocks of sheep,
            piles of clothing, and great
                quantities of other riches.
Straight back Minaya's pennant came, for
no one was fool enough to try
to tackle him from the rear. Straight
        back to Castejón and the Cid
           the raiders rode,
                loaded with all that plunder.
The Campeador rode out to meet his followers,
the castle left under guard.
He galloped forth to receive them with some of his men.
Arms wide, he welcomed Minaya:
                "You're here, Álvar Fáñez!
                hardy lance! No
                matter where I send you, I

never have to worry about it! What
you and I have added together of all the spoils, a
fifth of the whole is yours, if you will take it, Minaya."

24   MINAYA REFUSES ANY PART OF THE BOOTY, AND
MAKES A SOLEMN VOW.

"Esteemed Campeador, I thank you from the
heart, and this fifth you offer me is a sandwich
large enough to offer Alfonso of Castille. Let me
return it, give it up to you; and I swear to
God in heaven that I shall not accept even a
dull copper from you, until doing
battle with the Moors on the field, horseback,
with lance, with sword in hand, that I stand,
my arm stiff with blood above the elbow, before
Ruy Díaz, that illustrious fighter. No,
not a bloody copper. And
until I win you something that's worth something, all
the rest, I place it in your hand."

25   THE CID SELLS HIS FIFTH BACK TO THE MOORS. HE DOES
NOT WANT TO FIGHT WITH KING ALFONSO.

All the loot was gathered together.
The Cid thought: Alfonso.
He was sure the king would send an army out
to try to do him in. No.
He ordered that the plunder be divided and
let the partitioners keep a record of it.
His knights
found that they were prosperous, each got
one hundred marks of silver; to the foot, half of that unstinting;
the Cid kept one-fifth of the whole, which was normal.
He can't sell it in Castejón, or give it as a gift, nor

did he want to encumber himself with captives,
            men or women. So,
he spoke to the people of Castejón and sent
            to Hita and Guadalajara
            to find out
                how much they would pay for his share.
However much their proposition was, they
couldn't help but make a good profit.
The Moors bid three thousand silver marks,
            a bid acceptable to the Cid,
                and on the third day they laid
                    the whole amount on the line.
After a discussion with his men, the Cid decided that
there would not be room for all of them there in the fortress,
that it could be held, but that there was not enough water.
                "Let's leave the Moors in peace. Their
terms of capitulation to Castille are already written. King
Alfonso and his armies are certain to come looking for us. Listen,
        my men, Minaya, I want to leave Castejón!

26   THE CID MARCHES ON THE LANDS OF ZARAGOZA,
DEPENDENCIES OF THE MOORISH KING OF VALENCIA.

        "Don't be disappointed
        with what I'm going to say. We can't stay
        in Castejón. King Alfonso is too close, he'll
        be down here looking for us.
But I don't want to burn the fortress, I
want to free a hundred Moorish men, an
equal number of women,
so they will not speak badly of me,
            after all, I took it from them.
                All of you are paid,
                no one going short.
Since I don't want to fight with Alfonso, my lord, to-

morrow morning let's get this on the road."
Everyone was satisfied
with mio Cid's proposition.
They'd taken the castle
and were leaving it rich men.
All the Moors, men and women,
are blessing him.
                    Upriver along the Henares,
                        they go as far as they can, up
to the Alcarria region, continue past the Anguita caves, across
the Taruña River over
                into the Taranz Plain, to the
                        far edges of that country.
The Cid decided to camp between Ariza and Cetina.
Passing through these lands, he took
booty in plenty.
                    The Moors can't figure
                    the strategy of these horsemen.
                    Mio Cid de Bivar the next day
                            kept on the move, Alhama,
then La Hoz, then Bubierca, then Ateca and beyond.
Above Alcocer,
                mio Cid halted. He
settled for a rounded hill, a good strong position,
                    with the Jalón running nearby, the
                        water they couldn't cut off.
Mio Cid don Rodrigo
has decided to
take Alcocer.

27   THE CID CAMPS ABOVE ALCOCER.

Heavily he mans the hill, sets the tents strongly,
some against the mountainside,

some along the river.
The good Campeador,
who girded on sword in a good hour, gave the orders:
dig a trench around the base of the hill
near the water, so
secure the hill against surprise attack
day or night, and let the Moors know
that mio Cid has camped there, and
that he intends to stay.

28   THE MOORS' FEAR.

The news spread throughout all that country that
el mio Cid Campeador has occupied it, an
exile from the Christians, he's come among the Moors.
None of them dare to work the land
anywhere near the encampment. Mio
Cid and all his men are starting to enjoy it, for
the castle of Alcocer is going to pay them tribute.

29   THE CAMPEADOR TAKES ALCOCER BY STRATEGY.

The people of Alcocer now give tribute to the Cid,
and the people of Teca and Terrer and Calatayud,
though the latter paid grudgingly, it figures.
Fifteen weeks passed, and still
the Cid was settled there,
above Alcocer.
When he saw the town was not going to surrender, he
settled on a stratagem and wasted no time in trying it.
He struck all of the tents but one, left that standing,
and went off downriver, his banner lifted high, the
knights wearing their armor, their swords girt.
The whole trick was to draw

the Moors into ambush.
They saw the move in Alcocer, and
God, how they cheered!
"The Cid's provisions of bread and barley have given out.
He's struck all his tents but one, left but that one standing.
The Cid's heading off as though he were escaping from a rout.
The loot will be fantastic if we attack him now
before the people of Terrer get to him. If
they capture him first, they won't
leave us an empty basket.
The tribute he's taken from us, we'll
make him return twice over."
They rushed out of Alcocer at a speed
incredible indeed.
When mio Cid saw they were outside the walls, he fled
as from a rout. Down the Jalón he went,
his ranks all in disorder.
"There he goes!" they cried.
"Our prize is getting away!"
Large and small,
all raced out of Alcocer,
already smelling the capture,
thinking of nothing else,
leaving the gates behind them
open, and no one to guard them.
The good Campeador
swung his head around,
saw there was a good distance
between the Moors and the castle,
ordered an about-face, swung
the banner around, they spurred into a gallop.
"Hit 'em, men! Don't stop for anything!
With God's grace, they're all ours!"
The impact was met mid plain, God! how good the morning tasted!

Mio Cid and Álvar Fáñez spurred on ahead of the rest,
they had good horses, you can bet,
went as fast as they wanted. They
broke through the Moorish lines, then, got between
the Moorish lines and the castle.
Mio Cid's vassals laid it on without pity, in
a short space of time they kill three hundred Moors.
With great shouts, the troops
the Cid had left in ambush
cut in, left the front lines engaged,
and swung up toward the fortress,
drew up before the gates, naked
swords in their hands.
Then their companions arrived,
the Moors had been routed.
So you know now,
this is how mio Cid took Alcocer.

30   THE CID'S BANNER WAVES OVER ALCOCER.

Pedro Bermúdez came up,
the banner in his hand,
and set it at the very top,
the highest point of the fortress.
Then mio Cid Ruy Díaz, born in a good hour, spoke:
"Thank God in heaven and all his saints,
both riders and horses'll
have better quarters now.

31   THE CID'S MERCY TOWARD THE MOORS.

"Listen to me, Álvar Fáñez and the rest of you knights!
In taking this castle, we've taken a great prize.
I don't see many Moors that are left alive,

most of them are lying dead out there.
      The ones that are here, we
      cannot sell these men and women, and it
      would do us no credit to behead them. So
          now that we are lords of this place, let's
          take them in, and as we live in their houses,
            we can always use them as servants."

32   THE KING OF VALENCIA WANTS TO RECOVER ALCOCER.
HE SENDS AN ARMY AGAINST THE CID.

          With the spoils taken, el mio Cid
           is established in Alcocer.
He sent some men back for that tent he had left standing.
         The situation was very depressing in Ateca, and
      in Terrer no one particularly cheerful, and
everyone in Calatayud, you know it, walking around
with long faces. They sent a note to the king of Valencia
to the effect that, the man known as mio Cid,
        Ruy Díaz de Bivar,
          "exiled from the lands of Alfonso, came
and set up camp on a strong site above Alcocer. He
drew them into ambush and has taken the fortress.
If you do not come to our aid, you'll lose Ateca and Terrer,
         lose Calatayud as well, it
cannot escape; everything will go badly on this bank of the Jalón,
         and on the Jiloca side as well."
King Tamín of Valencia grew alarmed
      when he heard the message read:
          "I see before me here, three
          emirs:[3] two of you leave immediately,
          take three thousand armed men, and
      with those on the frontier who will help,
take this man alive and bring him to me.
For this invasion of my lands, he will answer to me."

Three thousand Moorish horse started out,
      reached Segorbe that night;
remounted the next morning,
reached Cella before nightfall.
They sent ahead letters to those along the border, who
      did not hesitate and began
          arriving from every direction.
The Moorish army left Cella,
the one called de Canal, rode all day.
    Without a pause, they rode onward, coming
    that night to Calatayud.
        All throughout that country, the call goes out,
        unbelievable numbers of men arrive to join
          the emirs, Fáriz and Galve.
They intend to circle and pin
the good Cid in Alcocer.

33   FÁRIZ AND GALVE BESIEGE THE CID IN ALCOCER.

    The tents are raised, the
    encampment built, the host,
already immense, is still growing. Among the Moors,
sentinels walk their posts in full armor, day and night.
      Outposts everywhere, the
      army is enormous.
Mio Cid's men are already short of water, and so cut off,
are bold and ready to sail out to battle. He firmly refused.
It had been three weeks now that they'd been firmly encircled.

34   THE CID HOLDS A COUNCIL WITH HIS MEN. SECRET
PREPARATIONS. THE CID RIDES FORTH TO DO BATTLE WITH FÁRIZ
AND GALVE. PEDRO BERMÚDEZ STRIKES THE FIRST BLOWS.

Three weeks were ended.
At the beginning of the fourth week,

the Cid turned to his men for a decision.
"They've cut off our water supply,
and the bread's about out. They'd
prevent us from getting away by night. Their strength is such
it would go heavy with us if we gave them battle. Gentlemen,
tell me, what would you like to do?"
                        Minaya, that useful knight, spoke first:
                        "Here in exile, we're not in sweet Castille;
                    if we fight, we'll get some bread from the Moors,
                damn sure, they're not going to give it to us.
        There are a good six hundred of us, maybe a few more,
in God's name, there's nothing else we can do.
Let's give them a fight, and let it be tomorrow."
                        Said the Campeador,
                        "Now you're talking like me, Minaya,
                        may you do yourself honor in action,
                        because that's what we're going to have."
He ordered all the Moorish men and women outside the walls,
so no one would know of his plans. All day and
all that night they spent in preparation.
                    By sunrise the next day,
                    the Cid and all his men
                    were armed and ready.
Then the Cid spoke, as you shall hear:
        "Let's all of us
            get into this operation, we'll leave
                just two of the foot to guard the gates.
                If we die on the field, then they'll get the castle.
                Should we gain the battle, we'll take
                        riches as well.
                Bermúdez, you take the flag, you're
a good man and will carry it honestly, but
no galloping with it until I tell you."
        Pedro Bermúdez kisses the Cid's hand

and seizes hold of the standard.

        The portals swing wide and they go charging out.

The Moors' sentinels see it, turn and run toward their troops.

How fast the Moors get cracking

and set to armoring up!

        Before the thunder of their battle drums[4]

           the earth wanted to crack.

You could watch the Moors seize weapons and

        double-time it to form the ranks.

There are two principal banners for the two emirs,

and such a melee of pennons among the frontier people,

who can count them? The Moors

      in battle lines

        more forward

          to take on the Cid and his men,

          hand to hand.

"Stand where you are, men, don't

budge from this spot. No one moves

forward until I give the word."

        But that Pedro Bermúdez

        can no longer stand it, he

has the Cid's banner in his hand, spurs off his horse, wheels about:

"God bless you, Campeador, I'm going to set this flag of yours

there in the thickest rank, then you'll see

that those who owe it fealty will

      rally to it!"

        "For the sake of charity, no!" cried the Campeador.

        Bermúdez answered, "That's how it's got to be."

Struck spurs to his horse and set the standard

down into the densest of the Moorish ranks.

The Moors meet him, try to capture the flag, deal him

      mighty blows, but cannot pierce the armor.

      "For the love of heaven, TO AID!"

        the Campeador cried.

35   The cid's men commit themselves to rescue
Pedro Bermúdez.

They bring their shields in front of their chests,
lower the lances into position flying their pennons, bend
their heads low over the fronts of their saddles and
charge to the fight, their hearts full to bursting with courage.
        In a great voice, he who was born in a good hour cried:
        "Cut them down, gentlemen, for the Creator's love! I
        am Ruy Díaz de Bivar, the Cid Campeador!"
They charge into the column where Pedro Bermúdez is,
three hundred
lances, each with its pennon,
            each struck through its mark,
             each took a Moor with it.
Rode out, turned and charged again,
        three hundred more were dead.

36   They lay havoc to the enemy columns.

        How many lances you would have seen
           go down and rise again,
        how many bucklers split and penetrated,
coats of mail breaking, cut to shreds, so many
            white pennons come out the other side,
            red with blood, how many
horses running without their riders!
The Moors cry out, "M A H O M E T!"
            and the Christians, "S A N T I A G O!"
In no time at all, one thousand
            three hundred Moors lay dead upon that field.

37   THE LIST OF THE PRINCIPAL CHRISTIAN KNIGHTS.

Settled into their gilded saddles,
what a good fight they put up!
mio Cid Ruy Díaz, that great warrior,
Minaya Álvar Fáñez, lord of Zorita,
Martín Antolínez, that worthy man of Burgos,
Muño Gustioz who grew up in the Cid's household,
Martín Muñoz who commanded Montemayor,
Álvar Álvarez and Álvar Salvadórez,
Galindo García, that excellent Aragonese,
Félix Muñoz, nephew of the Campeador!
These and how many others rush forward to
redeem the banner and el mio Cid Campeador.

38   MINAYA IN TROUBLE. THE CID WOUNDS FÁRIZ.

They killed the horse under Minaya Álvar Fáñez,
and a host of Christians quickly came to his aid.
His lance is broken, but he put hand to his sword, he
goes on dealing murderous blows, even though he is on foot.
The Cid saw that he was in trouble:
rode up to a vizir who had a good horse,
and struck him such a sword-blow with his good right arm
that he cut the Moor in half at the waist, and
half of him fell to the ground.
He led the horse over to Minaya Álvar Fáñez:
"Into the saddle, Minaya, you're my right arm
and I shall need you today for sure, the Moors
are still holding, standing firm on the field, we have to
try to finish them off."

Minaya mounted,
with sword in hand, dashes into the Moorish forces, fighting furiously,
        slaying everyone who gets near him.
    Mio Cid Ruy Díaz, born in a good hour, laid
    three blows on the emir Fáriz;
two of the strokes fail, but the third cuts through, and
the blood splashes out through the tunic of chain mail.
The Moor reins in
       and wheels his horse about
        to flee the field.
That single blow has turned the tide of the fight.

39   GALVE IS WOUNDED AND THE MOORS PUT TO ROUT.

Martín Antolínez dealt
Galve such a blow that
it split the great rubies on the emir's headpiece, cut
       through the helmet and reached flesh.
The Moor didn't wait around for a second blow, you know it!
Both the emirs down, Fáriz and Galve! a
       great day for Christendom,
for the Moors flee in every direction, and the Cid's men give chase,
        catch and cut them down.
The emir Fáriz got into Terrer,
but the people there
refused Galve protection, he
       headed for Calatayud
       as fast as he could move.
Ruy Díaz Campeador took off after him;
the chase lasted
       all the way to Calatayud.

40   MINAYA'S VOW IS FULFILLED. THE BATTLE LOOT. THE
CID RESERVES A PRESENT FOR THE KING.

The Moorish horse ran very well for Minaya Álvar Fáñez:
he killed thirty-four of those Moors. His
sword was keen and his arm
was red up to the elbow, drenched with blood, streaming.
     "My vow is paid," said Minaya, "and the news
     will reach Castille that
     the Cid Ruy Díaz has
     won on the field of battle."
Few Moors are left living, so many lie there dead.
In a pursuit without pause, the Cid's men cut them down.
               Now they return.
       The Cid was riding in on his fine steed, his
mailed coif gathered back on his shoulders, and the cloth cap pushed back,
          God, how splendid his beard!
          his sword held in his hand.
          He watched his men returning:
"Thanks be to God in heaven that we have triumphed in such a battle."
The Christian troops then sacked the Moorish encampment
of arms and shields and other objects of value. When
they'd rounded up the Moorish horses, they found
        they'd captured 510.
     Great joy ran among the Christian host, not
     more than fifteen of their men had been lost.
They brought in so much gold and silver they didn't know
          where to put it;
with the booty that had fallen to them,
         everyone was rich.
The Moors from Alcocer returned to the castle, and

the Cid ordered
even they should be given something.
El Cid and all his troops
    were joyful; he gave the word
      to divvy up the monies and
        all the other goods.
In his fifth part alone, one hundred horses fell to the Cid.
Splendid were the portions he paid out to all his vassals,
      knight and foot soldier alike.
So justly he divides it, that
all his men
are more than satisfied.
     "Minaya, my right arm, listen!
     Out of all this treasure God has given us,
     take with your own hand what pleasures you.
And it's you I want to send to Castille with
    the news of this battle we've won.
To King Alfons, whose anger is against me, I
want to send as gift thirty horses, all with saddles and
handsomely bridled, swords hung from the saddletrees."
    Minaya Álvar Fáñez said: "That,
      I'll do gladly."

41   THE CID FULFILLS HIS OFFERTORY TO THE CATHEDRAL
AT BURGOS.

    "Here's a boot filled to the top,
    overflowing with fine gold and silver.
Have a thousand masses said in Santa María de Burgos.
Whatever is left, give to my wife and daughters; ask
that they pray for me by day and by night, and if I live,
I'll give them enough yet to see them wealthy."

42   MINAYA LEAVES FOR CASTILLE.

Minaya Álvar Fáñez is pleased with the assignment;
the men are counted off who are to go with him.
Now they feed the horses, already night has come.
Mio Cid Ruy Díaz takes counsel with his men:

43   THE LEAVE-TAKING.

        "Well, are you off, Minaya?
        You can tell our friends there
that God was on our side and that we took the battle. If
        you miss us here on your return, follow it up,
you'll get to us somehow, the word will be around.
Swords and lances have to be our shelter here. In a
country like this with such poor pickings, no
other way to live, and as I see it,
        I'm afraid we'll have to leave it."

44   THE CID SELLS ALCOCER TO THE MOORS.

Everything set, Minaya set out the next morning.
The Campeador settled in with his men.
The countryside is poor and barren,
meager in its produce.
Every day,
the Moors of the frontier,
        and even some from beyond, kept spies on mio Cid.
        They were scheming something with the emir Fáriz,
          who'd recovered from his wound.
        But the people of Ateca and Terrer, and those
        of Calatayud, a more important town,

disposed of the matter together and set
the offer in writing. El mio Cid
sold them Alcocer
for three thousand marks of silver.

45   ALCOCER IS SOLD (*REPEAT*).

Mio Cid Ruy Díaz has sold the town of Alcocer;
every one of his followers receives a liberal share,
knight and foot alike, all are richer than before;
among all his vassals, you couldn't find a man that's poor.
He lives a life of comfort, who serves an openhanded lord.

46   ALCOCER IS ABANDONED. GOOD OMENS APPEAR. THE
CID CAMPS ON THE HILL ABOVE MONREAL.

When the Cid decided to leave the castle,
the Moorish men and women of the town began to groan and fret:
"Are you leaving us, Cid?
Our prayers go forth with you.
We rest pleased with how you've handled it."
As mio Cid of Bivar
left Alcocer, the Moors and their women commenced to wail.
He raised his banner and left, passed
down the Jalón, spurred onward; as
they left the course of the river, he saw
many birds of good omen.
Those of Terrer were pleased at the Cid's going,
even more the people of Calatayud, but
the Moors of Alcocer lamented, for he
had treated them honorably.
Mio Cid set spurs to horse,
passed onward still,
until he reached a rise above Monreal.
Lofty and large that hill,[5]

no one need fear attack from any side, and you know it.
He forced them to pay tribute at Daroca, to the north,
     and as far as Molina de Aragón, to the west,
        and even a third, Teruel, which is further south.
Even Celfa del Canal came under his hand.

47   MINAYA COMES BEFORE THE KING. ALFONSO PARDONS
MINAYA, BUT NOT EL CID.

Mio Cid Ruy Díaz, may God bless him forever!
     Álvar Fáñez Minaya went to Castille,
     presented the king with thirty horses.
       Alfonso smiled broadly when he saw them.
         "May God aid you, Minaya.
         Who has given us these?"
"Mio Cid Ruy Díaz, who girt on sword in a good hour!
     When you banished him,
       he took Alcocer by a ruse.
The king of Valencia sent word to surround him and take him.
When they cut him off from water,
mio Cid came out of the castle
and fought them in the field.
         In that fight,
       he beat two Moorish emirs,
       and the loot, sir, was enormous. He
     sends this gift to you, noble king, kisses
your feet, both your hands, and begs
mercy of you in the Lord's name."
Said the king:
        "very early in the morning to
       receive back into favor a man
       who's been exiled only three weeks.[6]
      But I accept the gift, especially if
        it's at the expense of the Moors; also,
it makes me happy to know that the Cid has taken such spoils.

Above all else, I pardon you, Minaya, and return to you
your rights and lands which were confiscated.
Go and come freely, I grant you favor as of now,
but of the Cid Campeador, I say no word to you.

48   THE KING ALLOWS CASTILLIANS TO JOIN THE CID.

"I would like to say moreover, Álvar Fáñez, that
I shall not penalize, either in their persons or in their properties, those
brave and valiant men anywhere in my kingdom
       who wish to go join the Cid."
      Minaya Álvar Fáñez kissed his hands:
         "Many, many thanks, O King, my lord from birth.
         This much you grant us today, more will come later.
We shall cook such dishes for you as will persuade you."
The king said: "You speak beside the point, Minaya.
Waste no more time, ride out through Castille, no one will stop you.
Go find the Cid."

49   THE CID'S RAIDS FROM EL POYO. TWO HUNDRED CASTIL-
LIANS WITH HIM, MINAYA REJOINS THE CID.

         I should like to tell you of him who in good hour
         girded on sword. He set up camp on that hill,
and while there are Moors and Christians left, it will say on the maps:
         El Poyo de mio Cid.[7]
From there, he raided much of that country, set
the whole valley of the river Martín under tribute.
News of the strikes went up to Zaragoza
      and didn't exactly please the Moors.
     The Cid spent fifteen weeks at El Poyo;
        and when he saw that Minaya was long overdue,
he took all his men, made an overnight march from that hill,
        leaving the camp deserted,

headed south of Teruel, and came to a halt
in the pine grove of Tévar. All the
countryside about there fell to his raiders.
He forced Zaragoza itself to pay him tribute.
So this went on, and at the end of three weeks,
Minaya rode in from Castille, two hundred with him,
all with swords,
and Lord knows how many foot,
a great number, in any case.
When Minaya came into sight, when the Cid saw him,
he threw his horse into a dead run, never
stopping till he embraced him, kissed him
on the mouth and on both eyes.
El Campeador smiled happily:
Álvar Fáñez reported candidly everything that had happened.
"Thanks to God and his holy graces,
as long as you live, Minaya,
nothing can go wrong for me!"

50   HAPPINESS OF THE EXILES TO RECEIVE NEWS FROM
CASTILLE.

God, how all that company rejoiced
that Minaya Fáñez was back!
bringing them word from brothers,
cousins,
all the families they'd left behind.

51   THE HAPPINESS OF THE CID (PARALLEL PASSAGE)

O God, how he is happy, with his handsome beard,
that Álvar Fáñez had bought a thousand masses, that
he brings greetings from his wife and from his daughters!
God, the Cid was glad and spread great cheer!

> "Ya, Álvar Fáñez, live many days!
>   Mission accomplished! You're worth
>   the rest of us put together!"

52   THE CID PLUNDERS THE COUNTRYSIDE AROUND ALCAÑIZ.

El Cid didn't wait around
but took two hundred knights,
chose them by hand himself,
                    and rode all night to the raid.
The fields around Alcañiz he leaves black behind him, plunders
                    the surrounding countryside.
          The third day, he turns around
and heads back to El Poyo.

53   PUNISHING THE MOORS.

News of the raid spread
through all those lands. The people of Monzón and Huesca,
               that far north, were troubled.
          The people of Zaragoza are happy,
they're already paying tribute, so need not fear
               the depredations of Ruy Díaz.

54   THE CID QUITS EL POYO. HE RAIDS COUNTRY THAT IS UNDER THE PROTECTION OF THE COUNT OF BARCELONA.

They return to camp with all the gain they'd got, all
               are happy with the great amount of loot;
          El Cid is elated, and Álvar Fáñez, too.
          The Campeador could not keep from smiling:
               "Boys, I have to tell you the truth,
                    miserable as it is:

if you stay in one place forever, well,
you can always beg for a living.
In the morning, we'll break camp, first
thing tomorrow, we're moving out of here."
So, mio Cid moved on, then, to the pass at Olocau; from there
he raided out as far as Huesa and Montalbán for the next ten days.
Word got around
that the exile from Castille was wreaking
a fair amount of havoc.

55   THREATS FROM THE COUNT OF BARCELONA.

The reports have spread in all directions, and come at last
to the count of Barcelona that
mio Cid Ruy Díaz
is overrunning all his lands,
which news weighs very heavily on him,
in fact, he's mad.

56   THE CID TRIES IN VAIN TO CALM THE COUNT.

The count is a big bag of wind,
so he said something windy:
"Mio Cid de Bivar is one large pain, in
my own court he committed
an intolerable offense, he
wounded my nephew and failed to make amends; now
he's raiding lands under my protection.
I never challenged him for that first offense,
or turned my friendship away,
but now he seeks me out,
I'll see I get satisfaction from him."
Great are the powers he can command,
and they gather quickly to him.

Between Moors and Christians, a
great number assemble under him,
        and set out to cut off el Cid, the good
        Ruy Díaz de Bivar.
Three days and two nights, still they rode,
and caught up to mio Cid in the pine grove of Tévar. They come
in such great numbers, they are sure they'll capture him.
        Mio Cid don Rodrigo,
        carrying great loads of spoils,
            is just descending a mountainside into a valley
                when the message comes in from don Ramón;
                having heard it out, the Cid sends back an answer:
"Tell the count to go easy, I
have nothing that belongs to him, he
should let me go in peace."
        The count's reply:
            "Not so! For the old insult
and the new one as well, he shall pay taxes, this
            exile from Castille will learn
                who it is
                    he comes around insulting!"
The messenger returned at top speed.
As soon as he heard it, mio Cid de Bivar
realized he couldn't get out
with anything less than a fight.

57   THE CID HARANGUES HIS MEN

"All right, knights, stow the loot,
get your armor on and your weapons loose, and quickly!
Don Ramón is going to give us a great battle, he
has such a mob of Moors and Christians with him,
he won't let us off with anything less than a fight.
If we keep on going, they'll only cut us off, so
                let the battle be here.

Tighten your cinches and keep your arms at ready. See?
They're coming down the mountainside all wearing britches,
their cinches are loose and the saddles are all low-cantled;
we'll ride better, our Galician saddles have high backs, and
we've leather shin guards over the britches.

    With one hundred knights we ought to thin those crowded ranks.
If you meet them with lances before they reach the valley floor,
for every blow you strike you'll empty out three saddles.
Try to take my prizes from me, will he?

    Ramón Berenguer will see today
      who it is he has come seeking
        in this pine grove of Tévar."

58   THE CID WINS THE BATTLE, AND TAKES AS PRIZE THE
SWORD "COLADA."

By the time the Cid had finished his speech, the men were ready.
Armed and in their saddles, they watched
the Catalan force descending the slope. When
they were almost to the bottom near the valley flats, the Cid
ordered the attack.

    The men responded with a will, using
      their pennoned lances so well that
while wounding some, they unhorsed still others.[8]
The man born in a good hour has taken the battle, taken
Ramón Berenguer, count of Barcelona, and won

    Colada, worth over one thousand marks.

59   THE COUNT OF BARCELONA A PRISONER. HE PREFERS TO
DIE OF HUNGER.

      Honor to his beard, he
      won this battle,
      took the count prisoner,
      led him to his own tent,

and ordered his faithful men
to mount guard over him.
The Cid left the tent and gave a leap, his
troops were coming in from all directions,
booty was plentiful, and the Cid pleased.
A great meal was on the fires for mio Cid don Rodrigo,
but the count don Ramón ignores it all.
They bring him food, set it before him,
he mocks them all and will not touch it.
"I wouldn't touch a mouthful for everything in Spain.
I'd rather I lost my body first and my soul next, for
having been beaten in a fight with such
ill-shod beggars."

60   THE CID PROMISES THE COUNT HIS FREEDOM

You'll hear what Ruy Díaz said: "Count,
come on, eat, eat this bread, drink this wine.
If you do as I say, you'll go free, if not,
you'll never see the Christian world again."

61   THE COUNT REFUSES.

"You eat, don Rodrigo, then relax and take it easy, I
choose to die. I want nothing to eat."
By the third day, they still cannot persuade him.
They are still occupied
dividing up the great spoils they'd taken, but
they cannot make him touch a piece of bread.

62   THE CID REITERATES HIS PROMISE TO THE COUNT. HE SETS HIM AT LIBERTY AND SAYS FAREWELL.

"Eat something, Count," the Cid urged,
"you'll never see another Christian if you don't eat,

and if you do and satisfy me, I'll turn you loose,
Count, with two of your noblemen, free, understand?"
   The count heard this and grew more cheerful.
   "Cid, if you do as you say, I
   shall marvel at your action all my life."
    "Then eat, don Ramón,
    and when you're satisfied,
    I'll set you free and two men besides.
     But what you have lost in the field
     and what I have won,
you may be sure I won't give back a plugged dinar.
I need all of it for the men
  who share my beggary with me.
We meet our needs by taking from you and from others,
and it shall continue as long
as it pleases our Father in heaven,
as I am a man living under the wrath of my king,
      and in exile."
   The count was happy and asked for water
   that he might wash his hands.
They fetched it in and gave it to him at once.
He sat down to eat with the two knights
   whom the Cid had freed.
    God, he ate with a will!
The man born in a good hour sat beside him, said:
    "Eat up! and if your eating
    does not give me pleasure, why,
    we'll not budge from here, we
    shall not part from each other!"
Then the count said, "Gladly eat very gladly!"
He and his knights fell to eating quickly.
It's a pleasure for mio Cid to sit there watching, closely,
because Ramón Berenguer moves his hands so quickly.
   "Please, Cid, have our horses ready,
   we're all set, and'll ride off at once.

I haven't eaten with such enthusiasm since
the day I was made a count.
The taste of this meal you've given me
will never be forgotten."
Three richly saddled palfreys they gave them,
and costly garments, cloaks of fur and mantles.
Count don Ramón took his place between the two knights, and
the Castillian rode out with them to say farewell
                    at the edge of camp:
            "Now, be off with you, Count, frank and free?
            You have my thanks for what you've left with me.
            And should you have any idea that you want revenge,
should you ever come looking for me, just let me know.
Either you'll leave some of your goods with me,
            or cart off some of mine."
                        "No danger of that, mio Cid, just forget it, I've
                        paid you enough to last me the whole year.
                        I've no intention of seeking you out again."

63   THE COUNT LEAVES DISTRUSTFULLY. THE WEALTH OF
THE EXILES.

The count dug in his spurs, rode off in haste.
He kept turning his head and looking back, afraid
that the Cid might change his mind—one thing
that mighty man would never do for all the money in the world,
for never in his life
                    had he given a treacherous word.
            The count is gone;
            el Cid de Bivar turns back,
            returns to his men.

He joins their celebration over the great and marvelous
      swag that they've taken. His men
      are all so rich, they hardly
      know how much they have.
           (Here ends the First Cantar del mio Cid.)

THE SECOND CANTAR

The Wedding of the Cid's Daughters

64   THE CID PROCEEDS AGAINST THE LANDS OF VALENCIA.

Herewith the story of mio Cid de Bivar
            begins anew.
He has withdrawn from Zaragoza and that territory,
left Huesa and the countryside near Montalbán, and
            occupied the pass of Olocau.
He began to do his soldiering against the coastal regions.
The sun rises in the east, that's where he went. Mio Cid
took Jérica, Onda, Almenara,
            the lands around Burriana, he has conquered them all.[1]

65   THE TAKING OF MURVIEDRO.

With the help of heaven, the aid of the Creator,
mio Cid took Murviedro, which showed him clearly
            that he had God's favor.
In the city of Valencia, there was more than a little fear.

66   THE MOORS OF VALENCIA SURROUND THE CID. HE
ASSEMBLES HIS MEN AND HARANGUES THEM.

The slightly more than somewhat alarmed Valencianos held
            a council, it figures,
                  and decided to go and besiege him.

They marched all night
     and when light came
          their tents
               were set up all about Murviedro.
The Cid saw them and was amazed:
"Thanks be to God our father!
We invade their lands, do them every mischief, drink
their wine, eat their bread—they've every right
          to come here and besiege us. We
          won't get out of this without a fight.
          Send word to those towns
          bound by treaty to help us, to
          Jérica, Olocau, Onda, to
Almenara, the people of Burriana, those towns,
bid them come here, we shall begin this battle, and
I trust, by God, we shall advance our fortunes."
By the third day
          They've all mustered together,
              and the Cid speaks:
                    "Listen men, and may God save you!
                    Since we left the cleanness of Christendom—not
          our pleasure, we had no choice—we've
          stayed ahead, thank God.
          Now the Valencianos have us hemmed in,
              and if we want to stay in this country, we
                 must teach them a hard lesson.

67   END OF THE CID'S SPEECH.

"Let night pass and the day come.
     I want
to see horses and men in readiness.
Let's go take a look at that army of theirs.
Like any exiled men in a strange land,

tomorrow we'll see
    which of you is worth his wages."

68   MINAYA GIVES THE PLAN OF BATTLE. THE CID WINS
ANOTHER FIELD. THE TAKING OF CEBOLLA.

Minaya Álvar Fáñez spoke, hear
what he had to say:
          "However you want it, Campeador,
we'll do it. But give me one hundred men, no more.
    With the others,
        you make the frontal attack,
good and hard and no mistake about it.
I'll come on from the rear with the other one hundred, and
        the field will be ours, I trust to God."
    His plan much pleased the Campeador.
    It was morning, almost, and they are arming;
each man knows exactly what he has to do. At dawn
        the attack began.
"For God and Santiago, knights,
hit them hardily and with love, I
am Ruy Díaz! mio Cid, el de Bivar!"
How many tent ropes you would have seen snapped in the Moorish camp!
        stakes wrenched out, tent poles, tents all
      over on their sides!
    But the Moors begin to recover, there are so many of them.
Then Álvar Fáñez rode in hard from the other side, and
though they hated to, they had to
        give ground, and pull out. On
foot or on horseback, those who can make it, escape. In the pursuit,
two Moorish emirs are killed. The chase went on, kept up,
      up to the gates of Valencia.
Mio Cid has taken great plunder, they
sack the camp, carry everything back to Murviedro.

The rejoicing in that town is enormous:
"They took Cebolla and land even beyond that."
"They're so scared in Valencia, they don't know what to do."
"The reports of mio Cid are being
circulated everywhere, and you know it!"

69   THE CID EXTENDS HIS RAIDS SOUTH OF VALENCIA.

His fame spread, even beyond the sea. El Cid
was cheerful, and so were all his troops, for
God had helped them in that great rout of the Moors.
They sent out raiding parties, rode hard all night,
getting to Cullera and Játiva, and as far south as Denia,
burst into the lands of the Moors
all the way to the sea.
They controlled the mountains of Benicadell,
the trails in, and
the trails out.[2]

70   THE CID IN BENICADELL.

When el Cid Campeador has seized
the passes of Benicadell,
it has them very worried in Játiva and Cullera, and
the distress in Valencia is unparalleled.

71   THE CONQUEST OF THE WHOLE OF THE VALENCIA
REGION.

Seizing and sacking, sleeping during the day, and
riding on raids at night,
taking those towns,

one after another, mio Cid
spent three years in Moorish territory.

72   THE CID LAYS SIEGE TO VALENCIA. HE SENDS WORD TO
OTHER CHRISTIANS, ASKING THEM TO JOIN THE WAR.

The Valencianos are humiliated, so scared,
          they dare not leave their gates,
                    much less meet him in battle.
He destroyed their orchards and ruined their crops
          each of those three years,
                    took bread out of their mouths.
The father cannot advise his son, nor the son his father.
Friend and friend
cannot console one another.
                    No easy thing, gentlemen, to
                    live on crusts of bread and see
                    sons and wives, to see them
                         dying of hunger.
Seeing only misery before them
they cannot alleviate, they
sent word to the king of Morocco. He
had such a great war going with the king of the Atlas range, that
he sent them neither advice, nor came to their rescue.
                    This news was a wind of gladness,
                    brushed over the Cid's heart.
One night, then, he rode the whole night long
          out from Murviedro, and had breakfast
               in the country around Monreal. He
ordered the news spread throughout Navarre and Aragón,
he even sent messengers back to Castillian territory:
"Anyone who wants to leave his miserable toil and acquire riches,

come to mio Cid, who has a taste for riding in Moorish land. He's
going to put Valencia to siege and give it into Christian hands.

73   REPETITION OF THE PROCLAMATION (*PARALLEL PASSAGE*).

"Whoever wants to come with me to besiege Valencia
—let every man come freely, I want no one with reservations—
                    in Cella del Canal, I'll
                    wait for him three days."

74   THOSE WHO ANSWERED THE CALL. THE ENCIRCLEMENT
OF VALENCIA. THE CITY IS TAKEN.

That was the message the Campeador sent out.
He returned to Murviedro which, as you know,
he'd already taken. The proclamations
                            spread to every part.
                    Somehow, no one wants to delay,
                    they smell loot, and
from all of Christendom men come and come. The word
spreads still, to every part of the land, more
flock to the Cid, and, you can understand,
                    no one deserted. His
                    stock is going up, mio Cid, el de Bivar!
             When he saw so many assembled, he rejoiced,
          and decided to wait no longer,
       he started for Valencia.
Mio Cid don Rodrigo is on the march!
He sets the siege so closely that there's no way out;
no kidding either, it's tight,
no one gets out or in.
He offered a term of respite so that
they could send for help, that someone come to their aid.

Nine months and no one came, you know? Nine months
                  he held them close.
Came the tenth, they had to give it to him.
        Great is the rejoicing there, when
              mio Cid took Valencia, entered the city.
Men who had been on foot made it into the city on horseback, and
as for the gold and silver, who could count it? All were rich,
as many of them as there were.
        Mio Cid don Rodrigo sent out for his fifth of the prize:
        in money alone, it came to thirty thousand marks, and
        as for the rest of the loot, who could answer?
            A day of great festivity for
          the Cid and all his men, when
        his lordly banner was flapping
from the citadel's highest tower!

75   THE KING OF SEVILLA TRIES TO RETAKE VALENCIA.

The Cid's troops and their commander
        were all taking it easy,
while the king of Sevilla³ was hearing that bad news.
        Valencia is taken, nothing to do.
          Well, something. He
            set out to attack it
              with an army of thirty thousand.
The battle was joined just beyond the orchards, and
mio Cid of the long beard
        beat them into a rout.
          The pursuit continued all the way
            south and into Játiva.
              You would have seen them sold very cheaply
              trying to cross the Júcar River.
            Moors in flight,
struggling against the current, having to drink

a good deal more water than they wanted.
The king of Sevilla escaped,
                         but carried three wounds with him.
El Cid returned to Valencia loaded with booty.
            When he had captured that city,
                 the spoils there were enormous,
                      so figure it, when the prizes from this battle
                           were larger still.
The share of the least of the foot soldiers amounted to one hundred silver
            marks. You
                      can imagine how his reputation spread
                           after this fight.

76   THE CID LEAVES HIS BEARD UNTRIMMED. THE WEALTH
OF THE CID'S MEN.

Among those Christian men who are
with mio Cid Ruy Díaz, the man
            born in a good hour,
            a party mood prevails.
                 His beard
is still growing and growing longer: mio Cid
had this to say about it:
                      "Out of love for King Alfonso, who
                           has sent me into exile, no
                      scissors shall ever touch it, or
                           one hair of it be cut, and
                      Moors and Christians alike shall speak of it."
            El Cid don Rodrigo takes his leisure in Valencia,
            Minaya Álvar Fáñez is constant at his side.
All those who came with the Campeador into exile
                      are rich now,
                 the famous Campeador gave all of them
                 lands and houses, they're satisfied, all

have tasted the Cid's love.
   Those who came to him later were
   also well rewarded, but the Cid sees
that if they could leave
with the riches they've already realized,
      they would leave with no compunction, so,
         as Minaya advised him,
the Cid commanded that no man who'd earned anything in his service
might go without first taking leave of the Cid, and kissing his hand,[4]
otherwise he'd be run down and, if possible, seized, all
         his goods taken from him and
            himself impaled on a stake. Having
seen that this order would be properly enforced, he
talks things over with Álvar Fáñez:
                  "What do you think, Minaya?
               I'd like to have a reckoning made up
                  of everyone here who's gotten some booty,
               to get it all down in writing and have
               all of them totaled up,
so that if any of them hide or we're missing anyone, his goods
shall be returned to me
         and that share forfeited
            to those old vassals of mine who
               are keeping guard around the outside of
                  the walls of Valencia."
"Wise counsel indeed," said Minaya.

77   ROLL CALL OF THE CID'S FOLLOWERS. HE DECIDES TO
SEND A NEW GIFT TO THE KING.

He ordered everyone to the court,
         and everyone came;
         and when they had arrived, he had them tallied:
            thirty-six hundred men had

                    mio Cid de Bivar,
                    which number warmed his heart, brought
                        a smile to his face:
"Praises be to God, Minaya, and
his mother Mary as well! It was
with fewer men than these we rode
out from the gates of Bivar!
You think we have riches now?
            Just wait!
If it please you, Minaya, and
not seem a hardship to you, I
would like to send you to Castille again, where we have lands,
            to my rightful lord, King Alfonso.
Out of my share of the prizes we've taken here, I want to send him
one hundred horses. You take them to him, kiss his hand for me, and
implore him to find the mercy in his heart to allow
that I bring my wife here, Jimena and both my daughters.
            I shall send for them, and this will be the message:
                'Mio Cid's wife and daughters will be given passage
                and will come with respect and honors
                    to these foreign lands
                which we have been able to win.'"
                    Minaya said: "With great pleasure."
Their talk finished,
they started the preparations.
The Cid detailed one hundred men to Álvar Fáñez
to serve him on the trip and to use
                wholly at his discretion.
He gave him one thousand silver marks to take to San Pedro,
            five hundred of which were to go
            to the abbot, don Sancho, directly.

78   DON JERÓNIMO ARRIVES IN VALENCIA.

While everyone was cheerfully attending to the preparations, ·
     an ecclesiastic arrived from France, a
        bishop, don Jerónimo by name.
     very learned and schooled in letters he was,
and as a warrior, either on foot or horseback, it
          would be hard to find a better.
He walked around asking for
     details of the Cid's deeds,
        breathing hard to get into the field
        against the Moors, declaring
that no Christian should bother to mourn him for the rest of all time
if he ever tired of fighting against them, hand to hand.
Mio Cid was delighted to hear it, and said: "Listen, Minaya,
by God in heaven, when the Lord sees fit to favor us,
let us be properly grateful:
     I want to make a regular diocese
        in Valencia and the lands about, and
          offer it to this good Christian.
You will take the good news with you, when you go to Castille."

79   DON JERÓNIMO IS MADE BISHOP.

Álvar Fáñez was pleased by what
don Rodrigo had said:
and everyone consented to
confer the diocese of Valencia
upon don Jerónimo, and
to endow it richly.
God, all of Christendom was happy!

Now there was a lord bishop in the lands of Valencia!
   Minaya was content as well, as he
     set out on his journey,
       made his farewells.

80   Minaya heads toward Carrión.

    Leaving the lands of Valencia lying in peace,
    Minaya Álvar Fáñez proceeded toward Castille.
    The names of the places he stopped, I'd rather
      not spend time to list.
    He asked for King Alfonso, where he might be found.
    The king had been at Sahagún not long before, but then
    had turned east, back to Carrión; might be found there.
Minaya was pleased to hear this, and
rode toward that place, bringing the gifts with him.

81   Minaya greets the king.

    King Alfonso
had just then come out from hearing mass, when
Minaya Álvar Fáñez arrived, most opportunely.
    Before all the people he knelt down on his knees,
    he fell with great sorrow at the king's feet, and
    kissed his hands, addressed him, spoke to the point:

82   Minaya's speech to the king. The envy of García
Ordóñez. The king pardons the Cid's family. The infantes
de Carrión covet the Cid's wealth.

"My lord, Alfonso,
out of love for the Creator, I beg your mercy.
Mio Cid, the warrior, kisses your hands, kisses
    your feet and your hands, his
    duty to so good a lord.

He begs you to grant him mercy, and may God protect you!
Exiled from his lands and deprived of your love, nonetheless,
    in alien country he has not done badly.
    He's taken Jérica and that town called Onda,
        seized Almenara, and
      Murviedro, which is even larger,
     also Cebolla, beyond that, Castejón
and the strong mountain range of Benicadell.
Besides all which, now he is lord of Valencia,
    and made an episcopate with his own hand.
The good Campeador has fought five pitched battles in the field
    and won them all. The prizes,
      believe me, were enormous, God
        was generous, and the proofs
         I have here with me.
           Here are one hundred horses,
good, fat, heavy ones, and fast,
every one saddled and bridled.
        He kisses your hands, begs
        that you accept them, he
        claims he is still your vassal, calls upon
        you, his lord."
The king raised his right hand and crossed himself:
    "May San Isidro protect me, I
    am pleased from the heart,
I am, with the mighty gains the Cid has made, and with
the news of what he has done, won, the Campeador, I
    accept these horses he has sent as a gift."
Though the king was pleased, García Ordóñez was not:
      "It would seem that there
      are no men left alive in
      Moorish territory, since
      the Cid Campeador does as he likes!"
"Not for you to say," the king told the count, "like it or not,
    he serves me better than you do."

Then Minaya spoke like a man:
>"The Cid begs your permission, if it please you,
>that you allow his wife, the doña Jimena, and
>both his daughters to leave the monastery,
>>where he has placed them,
>and to go to the good Campeador in Valencia."

The king said then: "It pleases my heart to do it. I shall
command they be given escort traveling through my lands,
and take care that no harm, affront, or dishonor befall them.
You and the Cid keep them safe when they are beyond my borders.
>Hear me, my vassals, and all my court!
>I wish the Campeador to suffer no loss.
>And as for all those vassals who call him lord, whose
>estates I confiscated for that reason, I
>hereby restore them everything, let them
>keep it all, wherever they go in the service of the Campeador.
>Their persons I free of harm,
>>assure them against injury, and
>I do this that they may serve their lord."

Minaya Álvar Fáñez kissed his hands, the king
smiled, and spoke with royal generosity:
>"Those who wish to serve the Campeador,
>I give them leave, may the grace of God go with you.
>We shall gain more by this than by continued rancor."

At this point,
>the infantes de Carrión[5]
>>discussed the matter between themselves:

"The fame of mio Cid el Campeador grows. It
would prove to our advantage to marry his daughters, no?
We would not dare, however, to advance the project.
Mio Cid is from Bivar, and we are
>from the counts of Carrión."

So they said nothing to anyone, and there the matter rested.
Minaya Álvar Fáñez bade the king good-bye:

"Are you leaving us now, Minaya?
May God's grace go with you.
Take a royal herald with you, I will see he provides you well.
If you take the ladies, care for them diligently, see
      they have everything they need, use my name, as
            far as Medinaceli.
From that point on, the Campeador will concern himself with them."
     Minaya said his farewells, and left the court.

83   MINAYA HEADS FOR CARDEÑA TO GET DOÑA JIMENA.
MORE CASTILLIAN KNIGHTS OFFER TO GO TO VALENCIA. MINAYA
IN BURGOS. HE PROMISES THE JEWS FULL PAYMENT FOR THE CID'S
DEBT. MINAYA RETURNS TO CARDEÑA AND LEAVES WITH JIMENA.
PEDRO BERMÚDEZ LEAVES VALENCIA TO MEET JIMENA. AL-
BENGALBÓN JOINS HIM IN MOLINA. THEY MEET MINAYA IN
MEDINACELI.

     The infantes de Carrión have come to a decision,
and ride some of the way with Minaya Álvar Fáñez.
      "You're worthy in everything, Minaya, be
      friend to us in this: give
      our greetings to mio Cid de Bivar; say
that we are on his side and will do whatever we can,
      he will lose nothing by our friendship."
And Minaya answered:
       "Your message gives me no reason
       to feel overburdened."
     Minaya has gone onward and the heirs of Carrión
turn back along the same road. Minaya heads straight for San Pedro
where the ladies are staying. When they saw him appear, how
great was their rejoicing! He
dismounts, and first prays to San Pedro; the prayer done,
      he turns to the ladies:
      "Humbly I address you, doña Jimena, may

God save and keep you and both your
little daughters from harm. And
greetings from mio Cid from where he is, I
left him in good health and prosperous.
The king, in his mercy, has set you free to go with me, so that
I can take you to Valencia
where we have quite a fief now. If
the Cid could see you well and unharmed, he
would be completely happy, and
would have nothing to worry about."
Doña Jimena answered: "As God commands it."
Minaya Álvar Fáñez ordered three knights to ride ahead,
to go to where the Cid was, in Valencia:
"Tell the Campeador—God keep him from harm—
that the king has released his wife and both his children
into my custody, and has
ordered escort for us while we are in his lands.
We'll be there inside of fifteen days, if we're lucky,
I, his wife and daughters, and as many of their serving ladies
as there are here."
The knights rode off and will take care of the matter;
Minaya Álvar Fáñez stayed behind
in San Pedro de Cardeña.
You'd have seen knights
arriving from all directions;
they want to come to Valencia to join
mio Cid de Bivar,
asking Álvar Fáñez to recommend them.
Minaya said, "That, I shall do gladly."
Sixty-five more knights have showed up so far,
aside from the one hundred he arrived with.
There was a good-sized escort to accompany the ladies.
Minaya gave the abbot the five hundred marks.
Now let me tell you what he did with the other five hundred:
he set out to buy

for Jimena, her daughters, and the ladies with them
the finest finery you could find in Burgos,
    along with palfreys and mules, so that
        they would make a splendid appearance.
When the fabrics for the ladies' attire was ready, and the
good Minaya was up and ready to ride back,
we see that Raquel and Vidas fall at his feet:
      "Minaya, worthy knight, have mercy on us!
    Unless the Cid comes through now, he's ruined us, and
            you know it. Let him
    give us back just the capital, and we'll forget the interest."
         "If God gets me back to Valencia, I'll
      speak with the Cid and see to it that
    you are well rewarded for what you've done."
    Raquel and Vidas said: "May
God grant it go that way. If not,
we'll leave Burgos and go all
the way to Valencia to find him."[6]
Minaya Álvar Fáñez leaves Burgos,
    goes back to San Pedro; many
      more men had gathered to join him, and he
      made ready to leave.
It was a sad parting they took of the abbot: "May God
avail you, Álvar Fáñez! Kiss the Campeador's hands for me.
This monastery asks that he not forget it; his beneficence toward us
will do him honor all the days of this world."
    "Glad to pass it on," said Minaya.
    Then, they make their farewells and ride off,
    the herald of the king with them to do them service.
Everywhere in the king's lands they were well taken care of.
It took them five days to get
        from San Pedro to Medinaceli.
         Now, the ladies and Álvar Fáñez
          have arrived in Medinaceli.
Let me tell you now of the knights

who went on ahead with the message:
Mio Cid de Bivar, at the hour when he heard it, had a
    great joy in his heart, turned to cheerfulness again,
        and these words rose to his lips:
            "A man who has the luck
                to send a good messenger,
                    has to expect good news. You,
Muño Gustioz, and Pedro Bermúdez, and you,
Martín Antolínez, worthy man of Burgos, and
my eminent cleric, bishop don Jerónimo,
take the road through Santa María de Albarracín to Molina,
take one hundred horsemen, armed as though for combat. Abengalbón
the Moor is lord in Molina and my friend in peace, he'll
take another one hundred men and go with you. Proceed, then,
straightway to Medinaceli, where you'll find, I'm told,
Minaya Álvar Fáñez and my wife and daughters.
Bring them here in all due honor.
I'll stay here in Valencia, which
has already cost me dear, and I'd be
mad to leave it unprotected. I
shall stay here in Valencia,
which is now my inheritance."
When the Cid had spoken, off they rode, pausing as seldom as possible.
They passed through Santa María, and stopped for the night at Bronchales
The next day they arrived in Molina, and when
the Moor Abengalbón heard of their coming, he
went out to meet them, showing great pleasure.
              "You've arrived, vassals of my true friend!
              I'm pleased to see you, believe me!" Not
              a man to stand on ceremony, Muño Gustioz spoke:
"The Cid sends you his greetings, and asks that you
provide one hundred knights to ride with us immediately.
His wife and daughters are now in Medinaceli.
He would like you to go there with us to escort them,

and not leave their side until we get back to Valencia."
Abengalbón said, "I shall do it gladly."
That night he spread a great banquet for them, and
in the morning they set out together. A hundred
knights had been asked for:
>   Abengalbón came with two hundred.
>   They enter the mountains of Luzón,
>   which are wild and high, pass over the
>   stony plain of Taranz,
so many of them that they feel no fear, then
descend by the Arbujuelo Valley.
>   A tight watch was being kept in Medinaceli, and
>   Minaya Álvar Fáñez saw the armed band approaching,
>   and was alarmed, sent out two knights to scout them.
They did not take long, for they had the courage.
One of the riders remained there with the band, the other
returned to Álvar Fáñez:
>   "Forces of the Campeador coming to find us:
>   Pedro Bermúdez is there, out in front, and
>   Muño Gustioz, your staunch friend,
>   and Martín Antolínez of Burgos,
>   as well as don Jerónimo, our steadfast bishop, and
the Moorish governor, Abengalbón, and his forces also, for
love of el Cid and to do him honor, all are riding together, and
they're coming now!"
>   Then Minaya said, "Let's ride!"
>   And so they did at once, with no delay, all one hundred ride out,
>   to make a good showing, riding good horses caparisoned
>   in silk, bells on all the harnesses, carrying
>   their shields hanging from neck and shoulder, their
>   lances high and the pennons streaming, so
>   that everyone would know that Álvar Fáñez had
>   acted with discretion and how he had escorted
>   the ladies out of Castille.

Advance detachments riding on ahead met,
they take up arms and fight for the fun of it;
they prance with great cheerfulness along the river Jalón.
    When the others arrived,
        they made obeisance to Minaya. When
           Abengalbón came up and set
              eyes upon him, he
                  smiled broadly, went to embrace him,
he kissed him on the shoulder, Moorish style:
        "It's a glad day when I see you, Minaya Álvar Fáñez!
And you bring along with you these ladies
whose presence honors us, the wife
of el Cid the warrior, and his own daughters.
    All of us must do you honor, for
        the Cid's fortune is such that,
           even if we should wish to hurt him,
              we could not do it.
              In war and in peace,
                  all we have is his, and
anyone who doesn't recognize the truth of this, well,
I think he's a fool."

84   THE VOYAGERS REST IN MEDINACELI. THEY LEAVE
MEDINACELI FOR MOLINA. THEY ARE ARRIVING NEAR TO
VALENCIA.

He smiled broadly, did Álvar Fáñez Minaya:
    "Abengalbón, you are an unfailing friend!
    God grant I see the Cid again, his soul alive inside him, you'll
have no reason to regret what you've done for him. Now, let's
        go rest,
           for supper's ready."
              Abengalbón replied, "I
am delighted with your hospitality. Within three days from now,
        I shall return it twice over."

They reentered Medinaceli
and all were highly pleased
with the provisions Minaya had made for their comfort.
The royal herald
ordered the costs
to be charged to him.
                    Though far off in Valencia, it
                    was in the Cid's honor,
            all the pomp and proceedings carried out in Medinaceli.
And Alfonso footed the bill, no expenses charged to Minaya.
                    The night passed and the next day is come,
                    mass is heard, then the journey is resumed.
They rode out of Medinaceli
            and crossed over the Jalón, riding swiftly,
            they moved up the Arbujuelo Valley, over
            the plain of Taranz,
and came at last to Molina, which Abengalbón commanded.
Bishop don Jerónimo, that sturdy Christian,
            guarded the ladies, day and night,
            and a good war-horse
            bearing his weapons,
            rode just ahead of him
                    to his right.
He and Álvar Fáñez rode together as a team.
They entered Molina, a goodly town and rich.
Abengalbón the Moor entertained them, nothing lacking,
            whatever they desired was provided. He
            even had some of their horses newly shod.
                    As for Minaya and the ladies,
                    Lord, how he did them honor!
At morning the next day, they continued the journey.
Until they reached Valencia, he served them royally, spent
all his own monies and refused to take
            anything from them.
With great rejoicings and these tidings of honor, they came

to within three leagues of Valencia.
Word was sent ahead, then,
to mio Cid inside the town,
to him who in good hour had girded on his sword.

85   THE CID SENDS HIS PEOPLE TO MEET THE TRAVELERS.

No other joy had ever been as great as mio Cid's,
he'd never been as happy as
at the coming of news about
the ones he loved best in the world.
He ordered that two hundred knights leave instantly to
greet Minaya and the noble ladies.
He, himself, remains in Valencia,
to guard the city and care for it, for
he knows that Álvar Fáñez is
taking every precaution.

86   DON JERÓNIMO RIDES AHEAD TO VALENCIA TO GET A
PROCESSION READY. THE CID RIDES OUT TO MEET JIMENA.
EVERYONE ENTERS THE CITY.

And look, how everyone's out there to receive Minaya,
the two girls, and the ladies! The Cid
commanded his men in the city to set guard over the citadel,
the other high towers, all the gates, the
exits and entrances.
And he had them bring his horse, Babieca, to him,
that, not long ago, he had seized
from the defeated king of Sevilla.
The Cid, who girded on sword in a good hour, had not
ridden him yet, and did not know
whether the horse was fast or well trained.
He wished to sport at arms before his wife and daughters

at the gates of Valencia where it would be safe.
The ladies were received with great honors.
The bishop don Jerónimo entered before them,
dismounted, went to the chapel and organized as many
clerics as he could gather who could get ready in time,
dressed in surplices and carrying silver crosses,
and moved the procession out to welcome
the ladies and good Minaya.
The man who was born in good hour
wasted no time:
he got into his silken tunic,
his long beard flowed loosely.
Babieca was saddled for him, decked out with trappings;
mio Cid rode out upon his back, bearing weapons of wood.
Upon Babieca, he charged out of the gates at a gallop,
it was a marvel to watch,
and when he had made the run in a long circle, everyone
was astounded. From that day on,
Babieca's worth was known throughout all Spain.
Having raced the animal, mio Cid dismounted,
and hurried toward his wife and daughters.
Seeing him approach,
doña Jimena
threw herself at his feet:
"Grace, O Campeador!
Bless the hour you girded on sword!
You've saved me many a sore trial, my lord,
and now you see me here with both your daughters.
God and your efforts be thanked, they're
good girls and well brought up."
He hugged the mother and both girls, all so happy that
tears ran from their eyes.
All his followers were
equally overjoyed, they

took up arms and tilted for sport and ran at targets
                    smashing the wood.
The man who in good hour girded on sword, hear what he said:
"You, doña Jimena, dear and honored wife,
and both my daughters, my heart and my soul,
come with me into this city of Valencia, into
this inheritance I've won for you."
                    Mother and daughters kissed his hands,
                    and entered Valencia with great honor.

87   FROM THE CITADEL, THE LADIES GAZE ON VALENCIA.

Mio Cid led the ladies to the citadel, took them
                    up to its highest point. They
cast their fair eyes in every direction, down over Valencia
            as it lay before them, on
                    one side the sea is visible, on
                            the other, fields and orchards, broad,
                                luxuriant, stretched out.
Their eyes look upon everything and find it pleasing.
They lift their hands to pray, to thank
God for this prize, it is so vast and good.
                    The Cid and his people lived a good, pleasant life.
                    Winter is gone and March about to come. Now I
                want to tell you news from overseas, and what
was happening with King Yúsuf
across the straits in Morocco.

88   THE KING OF MOROCCO COMES TO BESIEGE VALENCIA.

The king of Morocco was very worried
over mio Cid don Rodrigo: ". . . for
                            he has intruded brutally
                            into territories that are mine,

and gives all the credit to
no one but Jesus Christ."
And so that king of Morocco
mobilized his forces. Some
fifty thousand armed men comprised the striking force.
They embarked them all on ships and set sail to
strike at Valencia and to assail
mio Cid don Rodrigo. Now,
the ships have found harbor, and the men disembarked.

89   THE AFRICAN MOORS LAY SIEGE.

They have arrived in Valencia, the city the Cid has taken.
The unbelievers have set up their tents and settled down to the siege.
These facts had come to the Cid's attention.

90   THE CID'S HAPPINESS AT SEEING THE MOROCCAN
HORDES. JIMENA'S FEAR.

"Thank the heavenly Father and Creator, all
the goods I have in the world lie spread before me.
It wasn't easy to take Valencia,
now I hold it as my inheritance,
and won't let it go for anything short of death.
Thanks to the Lord and his mother Mary, my
daughters and my wife are here with me. That
all these have come from overseas, very satisfactory.
I've no choice, I have to take the field, and
my daughters and my wife can see me fight.
They'll see how you get a place to stay in a foreign country; with
their own eyes, they'll see how we earn our bread."
He led his wife and daughters
to the highest part of the castle,
from where their eyes could see the Moors

setting up their tents:
"God save you, what is happening, mio Cid?"
"My worthy wife, don't worry about a thing; a
marvelous great fortune has come to enrich us—
you've hardly gotten here and they want to send you presents—
the Moors have brought you dowries for the girls, see?"
"O thank you, Cid, and our Father in heaven."
"Wife, look, stay in this palace,
here in the citadel, and
when you see me in battle, don't be afraid.
With the help of God and the Holy Mother,
my heart takes strength because you're here to watch me, and
with God's help, I'll have to win this one."

91   THE CID REASSURES HIS WIFE AND DAUGHTERS. THE
MOORS ATTACK THE FARMLAND AND ORCHARDS AROUND
VALENCIA.

The Moors finish setting up their camp
and the dawn finally comes.
Their drums set up a faster beat, booming quickly.
Mio Cid was in high spirits, said:
"Ya, what a beautiful day!"
His wife is so filled with terror that she thinks her heart will burst,
her ladies and his two daughters
also are terrified;
since the day they were born, they'd never heard a noise like that.
He stroked his beard calmly, the good Cid Campeador:
"Don't be afraid, everything's in your favor;
before fifteen days are up, if it please the Creator,
we'll have those drums here in the house for you to play with.
We'll have them put before you, so you can see how they're made,
then give them to the bishop don Jerónimo as trophies
to hang in the cathedral of Santa María."

The Cid Campeador vowed this.
        The ladies lose their fear and grow cheerful.
Riding swiftly and without fear, the Moroccan Moors
pour into the farmlands about the city.

92   THE ONSET OF THE CHRISTIANS.

The sentinel saw it and rang the bell
        to sound the alarm.
Ruy Díaz's men are ready, they
arm themselves with a will and
are out of the city like a shot.
                        When they meet the Moors, they
                            close with them swiftly,
                driving them out of the orchards
                with an ugly ferocity.
They kill five hundred Moors by
the time that day is over.

93   THE PLAN OF BATTLE.

All the way
back to the tents the pursuit lasted, they've had
a hard and useful day and turn back to town.
                Álvar Salvadórez
                stayed there though, a prisoner.
        Those who had eaten the Cid's bread returned to his side, he
saw it with his own eyes, but they have to tell him about it.
Mio Cid is pleased with what they've done:
                "Now listen to me, men, this
                is the way it's got to go.
Today was a good day, tomorrow will be even better.
You'll all be armed before daybreak, don
Jerónimo, the bishop, will

give us absolution, he'll sing us mass, and
            then we'll ride out.
In the name of the Creator and Santiago, we'll
        hit 'em hard, forget there's anything else, either
                we'll take them, or they'll eat our bread."
                    Then everyone said, "You bet!"
                    Minaya spoke up hastily:
"As you say, Cid, but give me another tack:
give me 130 horsemen for this fight;
you hit 'em on one side, and
I'll come in from the other. God
will favor one or the other of us, maybe both."
        The Cid said then:
                "You've got it."

94   THE CID GRANTS THE BISHOP THE HONOR OF THE FIRST
BLOWS.

The day is gone
and night's come on,
and the Christian troops waste little time in preparation.
        At the second cockcrow before dawn, don
            Jerónimo sings the mass;
                the mass said,
                    he grants them full absolution:
"He who dies fighting today, face to face, in combat, I
hereby absolve him of all his sins, God will receive his soul.
As for you, Cid don Rodrigo, bless the hour you girded on sword,
I've sung this mass for you this morning, so now grant me a favor:
I want you to command me to strike the first blows in this fight."
                The Campeador said:
                    "It is so ordered."

95   THE CHRISTIANS SALLY OUT TO BATTLE. THE ROUT
OF YÚSUF. INCREDIBLE LOOT. THE CID GREETS HIS WIFE AND
DAUGHTERS. DOWRIES EVEN FOR JIMENA'S LADIES-IN-WAITING.
THE DIVISION OF THE SPOILS.

Armed to the points they all swarm out
by the towers on the western side of the city
by the Cuarto road; the Cid
gives his men last-minute instructions.
They make certain the men they leave to guard the gates
are very dependable, then they move out.
   Mio Cid leaped upon Babieca, the
   charger is decked out in all his trappings.
   Four thousand minus thirty with the Cid at their head
gallop out of Valencia, banner flapping, to
engage cheerfully fifty thousand Moors.
     Álvar Álvarez and Minaya
     strike from the rear.
God willing, they had the power to rout the Moors.
   Using his lance first, the Cid got his hand on the sword,
   he killed so many Moors you could not have counted them,
   the blood was streaming from the arm above his elbow.
   Three times he hacks at King Yúsuf, but
the Moor got his horse to moving and escaped the sword, took
refuge in Cullera, a palatial castle, at which
fortress the Cid arrived in hot pursuit with
whatever valiant vassals could keep his pace.
    The Cid, born in a good hour, turned back then,
very pleased with what they had taken in the chase, and
now knew Babieca's worth from head to tail. He
   has raked all those spoils into his hand.
A reckoning of the fifty thousand Moors showed

that only 104 escaped.
The Cid's men stripped the Moroccan camp:
they found three thousand marks in gold and silver mixed, and
there's no reckoning of the other prizes.
The Cid is jubilant and his vassals also
that God's grace has granted them the field.
When the king of Morocco was defeated in this way,
the Cid turned back to the city,
leaving Álvar Fáñez to see to it that all else was well in hand.
With one hundred knights, he returned to Valencia, helmet
and hooded coif off, his head naked, he
entered the city on Babieca, sword in hand.
The ladies, waiting there for him,
welcomed him back. The Cid
pulled rein and stopped before them:
"My homage, ladies, I've won great honor for you.
You held Valencia for me, and I won the field.
You no sooner arrive in Valencia, than God and all
his saints send us this enormous treasure.
You see my bloodied sword, and the horse lathered with sweat?
That's how we beat the Moors in battle.
Pray God he grant me some few more years of life, and you
will increase in honor, vassals will kiss your hands."
So saying, the Cid dismounted, and
when they saw that he was off the horse, the attendant ladies,
his daughters and his noble wife
knelt before the Campeador:
"We are in your gracious hands, may you live many years!"
They rose, and turned, and entered the palace with him, sat
with him there, on the elaborate benches.
"Now wife, doña Jimena, haven't you talked with me about this?
These ladies you brought, and who serve you so well, I
want to marry them to these vassals of mine, and give

two hundred marks to each of them. Let them know in Castille
who the lady was they served so well. As for your daughters,
   we shall come to that matter more slowly."
          All rose and came to kiss his hands,
          there was frolic throughout the palace,
          and as the Cid had promised, so it was done.
Minaya Fáñez was on the field
with all those men, counting and recording the loot.
The wealth of tents and arms was beyond belief:
let me tell you only the most important items.
There was no counting the number of horses running loose, and
    not enough men to round them up:
        even the Moors in the farmlands captured some.
Despite this, the share that fell to the Campeador included
one thousand horses of the finest and best-broken, and if
      so many fell to the Cid, the others
        were surely well paid.
    So many valuable tents and carved tent poles fell
      to the Campeador and his men!
The Cid ordered that one of the tents,
    the most lavish one of all,
      be left standing, and that
        no Christian touch it.
That was the tent of the king of Morocco,
supported by two tent poles worked with gold:
"A tent like this, come all the way from Morocco, I want
      to send to Alfonso the Castillian, so he can
        believe the news that the Cid has really made something."
They have entered Valencia with all these excesses of riches.
The bishop, don Jerónimo, the mitered man of merit, when
he had finished his hand-to-hand combats, he could not count
      the number of Moors he'd killed.
His share of the loot
was also enormous, for

mio Cid don Rodrigo,
man born in a good hour,

> sent him a tenth as tithe
> out of his own portion.

96   THE ELATION OF THE CHRISTIANS. THE CID SENDS A
NEW PRESENT TO THE KING.

> The Christians
> celebrate throughout Valencia,
> so many are their possessions, such
> a wealth of horses and arms.

Doña Jimena and both her daughters rejoice,
and all the other ladies who figure them-
selves as good as married.
The good Cid can't sit on anything for long:

> "Where are you, maestro? Come on over here, Minaya.
> For the booty that's your portion, you owe no thanks to anyone.
>> I mean it.
> Take whatever you want out of my fifth and leave the rest for me
> You leave tomorrow morning without fail, taking
> horses from this portion that I've earned, make sure
> each has saddle and reins, and each is equipped with a sword.
> And these two hundred horses are to go as gifts to Alfonso
> so that he will not speak badly of the lord of Valencia.
> And make this gift in my wife's name, and in the names of my daughters,
> that he sent them here, as he did, to where they are at ease. . . ."

He ordered Pedro Bermúdez to accompany Minaya.
They rode out early the next day,
two hundred men in their company,
with greetings from the Cid and to say

> that he kissed the king's hands,

sending as gift these two hundred horses from this battle the Cid had won,
"and I must serve him always,

> until my soul and body are no longer one."

97   MINAYA TAKES THE GIFT TO CASTILLE.

They have left Valencia
            and set out on their journey.
                        They carry such riches with them, they
                                    are constantly on guard.
Not stopping to rest, they rode
days and nights without stopping,
            past the range of mountains[7] that marked the border of
                        that other country, and began to ask about
                                    the whereabouts of Alfonso.

98   MINAYA GETS TO VALLADOLID.

Passing the ranges, the mountains and rivers, they
            arrive in Valladolid,
                        where King Alfonso was then;
Pedro Bermúdez and Minaya sent a message,
            asking him to welcome the company in,
                        for mio Cid de Valencia
                                    had another gift for him.

99   THE KING RIDES OUT TO WELCOME THE CID'S MEN. THE
ENVY OF GARCÍA ORDÓÑEZ.

The king was happy, you've never seen him so pleased.
He ordered all his nobles to horse, was himself among
            the first to dash out to see the messengers
                        come from him who was in good hour born, and
the infantes de Carrión did some second-guessing about that,
            which figures, as well as the Cid's worst enemy,
                        count don García—you can't please everybody.
They caught sight of the Campeador's men,
you would have thought they were an
army, not emissaries, and

King Alfonso kept making the sign of the cross.
>Minaya and Pedro Bermúdez arrived before them,
>leaped to the ground from their horses, knelt
before King Alfonso, they kiss the earth and both his feet:
"Grace, King Alfonso, be honored forever! We
kiss your feet in the name of Cid Campeador, he
>calls you lord, holds himself your vassal,
>and prizes highly the favor you have shown him.
A few days ago, O King,
he was victor in a battle against that king of Morocco,
>Yúsuf by name, fifty thousand with him, and he
>drove them from the field.
>He took enormous spoils, and
all his vassals have grown rich. Now he conveys these
two hundred horses to you, and kisses your hands."
>King Alfonso said:
>"I accept them with pleasure, and
>I thank mio Cid for such a gift as he has sent.
>May he see the hour when I can repay him for it."
This pleased many present, and they kissed his hands.
But it got to count don García, who grew furious,
>and rode off to one side with ten of his relatives:
"What a phenomenon, this Cid,
his credit always increasing. He
conquers kings in battle as easily
as if he found them lying there and led their horses away.
If he keeps this up, we re going to be in trouble."

100   THE KING SHOWS HIMSELF BENEVOLENT TOWARD THE CID.

You will hear now what King Alfonso said:
>"Thanks be to God and to Sant Isidro
>for these two hundred horses the Cid has sent.

In my time to come as king, I shall
expect even more of him. And to you,
        Minaya Álvar Fáñez and Pedro Bermúdez here, I
            command that you choose rich garments,
                outfit yourselves with whatever weapons please you,
            so that you may present a good appearance before
    mio Cid Ruy Díaz.
And here are three horses, take them now.
I say it willingly, that it seems clear to me
good things must follow from these new exploits."

IOI   THE INFANTES OF CARRIÓN INTEND TO MARRY THE
CID'S DAUGHTERS.

Bermúdez and Minaya kissed his hands
and went in to rest up a bit.
            Whatever they needed, he ordered that
                it should be provided for them.
                    Now, I want to tell you of
the heirs of Carrión holding their private discussions:
            "The Cid is doing very well indeed. Let us
            ask for his daughters in marriage, it'll
            be to our honor and we'll find ourselves
                on the way up!"
So they come to King Alfonso with this suggestion:

IO2   THE INFANTES CONVINCE THE KING TO ARRANGE THE
MARRIAGE FOR THEM. THE KING ASKS TO SEE THE CID. MINAYA
RETURNS TO VALENCIA AND TELLS THE CID THE WHOLE
BUSINESS. THE CID FIXES THE PLACE OF THE MEETING.

"O King and our lord, we ask a favor of you, that
        by your leave, we want you to ask
for the hands of the Cid's daughters for us,

we wish to marry them, for both his
honor and our advantage."
For a long hour, the king sat and meditated:
"The good Campeador,
I threw him out of the country,
did him harm, and he
has labored mightily for me.
I don't know if he'll find the marriage to his liking, but
since you're so eager for it, let us start negotiations."
Then the king don Alfonso sent
for Pedro Bermúdez and Minaya Alvar Fáñez,
took them into a room aside:
"Now listen, Minaya, and you, Pedro Bermúdez,
mio Cid Ruy Díaz Campeador serves me well,
he merits it and shall have from me full pardon,
and if it suits him, let him come and see me.
There's been another development here, in my court:
Diego and Fernando, the infantes de Carrión, have
in mind to marry his two daughters.
Be good messengers, and I beg you both to
convey all this to the good Campeador.
He'll have honor from it, and that honor will increase
by union with the family of the infantes de Carrión."
Having consulted with Pedro Bermúdez, Minaya spoke:
"We shall put it to him, just as you have said it,
then the Cid may do whatever pleases him."
"Tell Ruy Díaz I shall meet him
at any suitable location:
wherever he says,
let the mark be there.
However I can, I want to act to his advantage."
With that, they took leave of the king,
and they and all that were with them
returned to Valencia.

When the Cid heard they were coming,
he saddled up and rode out to meet them.
Mio Cid smiled, and hugged them warmly:
    "You're back, Minaya! and you, Pedro Bermúdez!
    Two such knights are hard to find in any country.
What's the word from my lord Alfonso? Was he
pleased? Did he accept the present?"
    Said Minaya:
"With heart and soul, he's pleased and sends his love."
    "God be thanked," said Ruy Díaz.
With that over, they began to tell him
what Alfonso de León had asked, that
he give his daughters to the heirs of Carrión, that
the king recommended the match with heart and soul,
that the Cid would increase his name and honor by it.
    When the good Campeador heard this,
    he thought and meditated a long while:
    "Thanks be to Christ the Lord for all this.
    They exiled me, took away all my possessions,
what I have now, I've gotten by
great and persistent toil;
that I have the king's favor, I thank God, and that he asks me for
my daughters for the heirs of Carrión. But tell me, Minaya,
    and you, Pedro Bermúdez,
    this marriage, how does it look to you?"
"We say, whatever pleases you."
    The Cid said:
    "They have a great name, these heirs of Carrión,
they are very proud and hold a good position in the court.
This marriage would not be to my liking.
But since he who is worth more than we advises it,
let us talk of the matter privately among ourselves.
I trust God in heaven will give us the right decision."
    "Another thing," said Minaya, "besides all this,

Alfonso said he would come to meet you where-
ever you liked, but he
                    wants to see you personally and
                    formally show his favor,
                    and you could decide after that
                    the best thing to do."
Then the Cid said,
                "This pleases me in my heart."
"About the meeting, then," said Minaya,
"better decide where you want it to be."
                "It would not have been a surprise
            if Alfonso had bid me to find him wherever he was,
        and I would have gone
to do proper honor to my king and lord.
But whatever he wishes, let his pleasure be ours.
On the Tagus, then, that's a major river, the
meeting will be there—let my lord set the day."
                They wrote letters, then, and sealed them tight,
                    sent them off by two knights. What
                        the king wants, the Campeador will do.

103   THE KING FIXES THE DAY OF THE INTERVIEW. HE GETS
HIS RETINUE READY TO GO.

The messengers, then,
they cast the letters before the worthy king.
        When he looked at them,
            it pleased his heart:
                "My greetings to mio Cid, who
                in good hour girded on sword! Our
                meeting will be three weeks from today.
                    If I'm alive, I'll
                    be there without fail."

They didn't delay an instant, but
    returned to mio Cid.
Both parties began to assemble
their resources for the meeting.
Who in Castille had ever seen so many
priceless mules, well-paced palfreys, so many
war-horses that were heavy, swift, surefooted? And no one
had ever seen so many fine pennons
    flying from sturdy lances,
        shields braced at the center with
            gold and with silver, cloaks and furs,
                and silks from the island of Andros.
The king ordered abundant provisions be sent
to the conference site on the Tagus. A great
and goodly company is to go with the king.
    The infantes de Carrión trot about cheerfully,
        borrowing in one place,
           spending in another, as
though their incomes had already increased that much and
they had all the gold and silver they could wish for.
                The king don Alfonso mounted up
            quickly, and
          with him counts, governors, magis-
        trates, and a great host of nobles.
    The infantes de Carrión also
brought along a sizable following.
With the king rode men of Galicia and León, and you can bet
no one could count the number of Castillians. Then all of them
let the reins loose and headed for the conference.

104   THE CID AND HIS MEN PREPARE TO GO TO THE MEETING.
THEY LEAVE VALENCIA. THE KING AND THE CID MEET ON THE
BANKS OF THE TAGUS. THE KING GIVES A SOLEMN PARDON TO

THE CID. INVITATIONS. THE KING ASKS THE CID FOR HIS DAUGH-
TERS, TO MARRY TO THE INFANTES. THE CID CONVEYS HIS
DAUGHTERS TO THE KING, WHO MARRIES THEM. THE CON-
FERENCE ENDS. THE CID'S GIFT TO THOSE WHO ARE LEAVING. THE
KING GIVES THE INFANTES INTO THE CID'S CHARGE.

Back at Valencia, mio Cid el Campeador
was not wasting time, but also
preparing for the meeting.
Many big mules for carrying and swift palfreys for the road,
so many splendid weapons, and so many fast war horses,
capes, mantles, and furs were readied, and
young and old, all dressed in colored garments.
   Minaya Álvar Fáñez and
   that same Pedro Bermúdez,
   Martín Muñoz, lord of Montmayor,
   Martín Antolínez, the old pro from Burgos, and
   bishop don Jerónimo, no better man was mitered,
   Álvar Álvarez and Álvar Salvadórez,
   Muño Gustioz, that very excellent rider,
   Galindo García, who came from Aragón,
   everyone got ready
to go with el Campeador, and all others, however many
and whoever they are.
   But the Campeador ordered two men,
   Álvar Salvadórez and Galindo García,
   the one from Aragón, to stay behind
and guard Valencia with all their powers.
And all the others who remained there were
to be under the orders of these two.
    The citadel gates, and
    mio Cid ordered it so, were
   to stay closed night and day. His wife
and both his daughters are inside there,
and there his heart and soul both are,

and other ladies besides who do their bidding.
So he made it very clear and strict indeed,
the man in good hour born, that
none of the ladies should leave the Alcázar, the
      fortress, until he returned.
              They rode forth from Valencia, set
              spur to horse,
each with a war-horse fast and strong at his right hand,
chargers the Cid had won on the field of battle—they
        certainly weren't gifts—and in this way
           proceeded toward
      the conference with the king as scheduled.
      The king don Alfonso arrived a day early.
      When he saw that the good Campeador was coming,
to do him honor, he led some men out to welcome him.
The Cid saw Alfonso coming and
commanded his men to halt, except those few knights
he loved best.
      With these fifteen he dismounted as he had planned.
          On hands and knees he knelt upon the earth,
          took the grass of the field in his teeth,
          weeping, he was so overjoyed;
      in this way he rendered obeisance to Alfonso his lord,
          and in this way fell at his feet.
      Alfonso was embarrassed at the sight:
"Ya, Cid Campeador, get up on your feet.
Kiss my hands, but do not kiss my feet,
if you do, you will lose my favor."
      The Campeador stayed on his knees:
      "I beg you mercy, my rightful lord! Like this I beg,
      grant me your favor that everyone here
          may witness and hear it."
The king said: "That I shall do with all my heart and soul,
          I hereby pardon you and grant you my love,
and from this day forward be welcome anywhere in my kingdom."

The Cid spoke and made this reply:
>"Thank you, I accept the pardon, my lord Alfonso,
>>I thank God in heaven for it, and afterward you
>>>and all these vassals standing about us."

Still kneeling, he kissed his hands, and then,
rising, he kissed him on the mouth.
>All the rest there were pleased to see it, except
>>Álvar Díaz and García Ordóñez, who were sorely annoyed.
>>>The Cid spoke then: "God the Father be thanked, for
>>>I have the favor of Alfonso, my lord, and
>>>>now God will defend me day and night. And
>>>>now, my lord, if it please you, be my guest."

The king replied: "Today that would not be proper,
you have only just arrived, and we came in last night.
>You'll be my guest today, Cid Campeador, and
>>tomorrow we'll do whatever you like."
>>>The Cid kissed his hand and deferred to him.

Then the infantes de Carrión came over to
>pay their respects:
>>"We salute you, Cid,
>>you were born in a good hour! We
>>shall work for your fortunes in any way we can."
>The Cid answered, "God grant it so!"

Mio Cid Ruy Díaz, the man born in a good hour, was
>that day the guest of the king, who was so fond of him
>>he couldn't get enough of his company, and who
>>>kept his eye on the great beard
>>>>which had grown very long by this time.
>>>>Indeed,
>>>>>the Cid was a marvel to look at
>>>>for everyone who was there.

>So the day went, and the night came on.
>The next day the sun rose bright and clear.

The Campeador ordered his camp to prepare

a meal for everyone there. And
mio Cid Campeador treated them all so well that
everyone was merry and glad to agree
that they hadn't eaten better in the last three years.

As the sun rose the morning of the following day, the
bishop don Jerónimo sang the mass.

Coming out from mass, they all crowded together;
the king waited no longer, but began his speech:
"Listen to me, my vassals, counts, and nobles,
I wish to bring up a matter with mio Cid Campeador,
and may Christ grant that it be to his profit.
I want to ask you for your daughters, doña Elvira and doña Sol,[8]
I want you to give them as wives to the infantes de Carrión.
The marriage appears to me honorable and to your advantage;
the infantes seek it of you, and I endorse it. May
everyone here, your men and mine,
on both sides, second this suit;[9]
give us your daughters, mio Cid, and may God reward you!"

"I've no daughters of marriageable age," the Cid replied,
"they're not very old, still children for that matter.
The renown of the heirs of Carrión is
great enough for my daughters, even
for others of higher station.
I'm their father;
both of them grew up in your court. Their
future and mine are both at your command. So,
I give doña Elvira and doña Sol into your hand; give them
to whomever you think best, I shan't complain."

"Thank you and thanks to all this court," the king replied.
Then the heirs of Carrión rose and went
to kiss the hands of the man born in a good hour, and
before king don Alfonso they exchanged swords.[10]
King Alfonso spoke as a good lord. "Thanks, Cid,
and thank God first of all, that you've

given me your daughters for the heirs of Carrión,
      you're a good man. Now,
I here take them into my hands, doña Elvira and doña Sol,
and give them as veiled in marriage to the infantes de Carrión.
With your love and consent I marry them, and may it please the Lord
      that good come of it. Herewith,
      I place the heirs of Carrión in your hands,
      they'll go with you, I am turning back here.
      I'm giving them three hundred marks in silver which
      you can put on the cost of the marriage or
      whatever you like or think fit. In
Valencia, that great city, they will be under your protection, all
      four, your sons-in-law and daughters,
      now all of them are your children.
      Do with them what pleases you, Campeador."
Mio Cid received the monies, and kissed Alfonso's hands:
"I thank you deeply, my lord and king.
It is you who give my daughters now in marriage,
not I."
      The words are set, the politenesses exchanged.
      They decide that at sunup next morning
the two parties will return to where they started. Then,
mio Cid, el Campeador, did something that would last in the news
for a long time;
      he began to hand out as gifts so many of those
      sturdy mules, fine palfreys, and those beautiful,
      costly garments he'd brought with him, to
whoever wanted them; anyone who asked for anything, no
one got "no" for an answer.
      Of the horses, the Cid
      gave sixty of them as gifts.

As many men as there were there, no one
went away from the meeting dissatisfied.
Night had come, it was time to leave.
The king took the hands of the heirs of Carrión and
put them into the hands of mio Cid Campeador:
"Since they are now your sons-in-law,
here are your sons. Know that
from today forward, they'll do what you want, Campeador.
Let them serve you like a father, and honor you as a lord."
                    "Thank you, my king, and I accept your gift.
                    May God in heaven grant you the
                    good reward you deserve.

105   THE CID DOES NOT WANT TO GIVE HIS DAUGHTERS
AWAY HIMSELF. MINAYA WILL BE THE KING'S REPRESENTATIVE.

            "May I ask you a favor, my king? Since
            you marry my children to suit yourself,
since you've taken charge of them,
would you designate someone to give them away in your name? I
will not give them away
with my own hand,
the heirs will not congratulate themselves that way."
                    The king replied, "Here comes Álvar Fáñez,
                        let him take them in his hands, and
                            give them to the heirs,
                as though he were I, taking them from a distance,
                as though they were here in our presence.
                Álvar Fáñez, you be their godfather all
                    through the ceremony,
                and tell me how it went, when next

we see one another."
Álvar Fáñez answered,
"That would please me, my lord."

106   THE CID TAKES LEAVE OF THE KING. PRESENTS.

All the pledges were sealed in great solemnity. "Ya,
King Alfonso, my most honored lord,
from our meeting you must take away something of mine.
I brought here for you thirty palfreys, they're well trained, and
thirty swift war horses, all with fine saddles. Please,
take these from me, and I kiss your hands."
Alfonso said, "You overwhelm me,
but I accept this gift you have given me. May it
please the Creator and all his saints
that you be well rewarded
for the pleasure it gives me.
Mio Cid Ruy Díaz,
you have honored me greatly and served me, and I
am pleased with you. If I live,
I'll manage to repay you some way!
Now, the Lord be with you, it's
been good to see you again.
May God in heaven see to it that everything works out well!"

107   MANY OF THE KING'S TROOPS GO WITH THE CID TO
VALENCIA. THE INFANTES ARE ACCOMPANIED BY PEDRO BERMÚDEZ.

The Cid leaped on his horse, Babieca:
"I say here,
before my lord, King Alfonso: if anyone here
wants to attend the wedding and
receive something as gift from me, let him
come with me now, I'll see that he profits from it."
Mio Cid took leave of Alfonso his lord,

for he did not wish to be escorted,
      but rode off then and there.
You'd have seen many footloose knights come up,
kiss King Alfonso's hands and take their leave:
      "Your grace, lord, and grant us leave and pardon,
          we shall go with the Cid's powers to
            great Valencia, to be
              present when the infantes de Carrión
          wed the Cid's daughters,
        doña Elvira and doña Sol."
      The king was glad and released them all. As the
company of the king decreased, so that of the Cid grew, many
          people went with the Campeador.
So they set out for Valencia, the city he had won.
Pedro Bermúdez and Muño Gustioz:
in all his company, the Cid did not have two better men.
      He had them ride with Fernando and Diego, to
        learn the dispositions of the heirs of Carrión.
Ansur González went with them, a troublemaker and loudmouth,
        not being good at much else.
They showed the greatest respect for the infantes de Carrión.
      Now they reach Valencia which the Cid has taken.
      The closer they got to the city, the more
        their spirits soared.
Mio Cid spoke to don Pedro and to Muño Gustioz:
        "See to the heirs' lodgings, and
        stick with them, that's an order.
        In the morning when the sun has hurled
        itself into the sky, they'll see
        their wives, doña Elvira and doña Sol."

108   THE CID TELLS JIMENA ABOUT THE MARRIAGE.

      Everyone went to his quarters for the night.
Mio Cid Campeador went to the fortress and was

received by Jimena and both his daughters.
     "You're back, Campeador! a good hour
     you girded on sword! May we
     look upon you many days with these eyes of ours!"
"Yes, I'm back, dear wife, God be thanked, and I've
     brought with me two sons-in-law
       in whom we shall have much honor.
Now, say 'thank you,' daughters, for I've married you well!"

109   DOÑA JIMENA AND HER DAUGHTERS APPEAR PLEASED.

     His wife and his daughters, they kiss his hands,
     so do all the ladies-in-waiting.
"Thanks to the Creator, and to you,
     Cid of the marvelous beard, you
       cannot do anything wrong! They'll
         lack for nothing all the rest of your days!"
"When you marry us off, Father, will we really be rich?"

110   THE CID'S MISTRUST OF THE MARRIAGE.

"I'm thankful to God, I'll tell you that, Jimena.
And to you, daughters, doña Elvira and doña Sol, it's so,
we shall increase in honor from this marriage of yours.
But I want you to know the truth, it wasn't I who carried it off.
My lord Alfonso asked me for you, was
     such an insistent petitioner,
       and with all his heart,
there was no way I could have said him 'no.' So,
I gave you, both my daughters, into his hands, so that now
it's he who is marrying you, not I,
you'd better believe it."

III   WEDDING PREPARATIONS. THE PRESENTATION OF THE
INFANTES. MINAYA GIVES THE WIVES AWAY TO THE HEIRS.
BENEDICTIONS AND MASSES. A TWO-WEEK FIESTA. THE WEDDING
FESTIVITIES END: THE GUESTS GET GIFTS. THE SINGER BIDS HIS
AUDIENCE FAREWELL.

They began then
to get the palace ready;
floors were covered and the walls hung
with purple fabric, silks, and other
rich material.
It was a pleasure to sit down and eat in that place. All
the knights assembled quickly, then
the heirs of Carrión are sent for.
The infantes clamber onto their horses and head for the palace,
all done up in their best finery.
With the good taste to approach on foot, they came in,
all decorum and seemly.
Mio Cid and his vassals all welcomed them;
they bowed humbly before him and his wife, and went to sit
on a beautifully carved bench.
The Cid's men,
discreet and steady, are
sitting and waiting
for him, born in a good hour,
to speak.
The Campeador got to his feet:
"Well, we have to do it, what
are we waiting for?
Álvar Fáñez, come over here,
you whom I love best, here I
give both my daughters into your hands.

You know that the king has named you, and I promised him it would be so,
I do not want in any way to fault what has been settled.
Give them to the infantes de Carrión with your own hand,
let them take the benediction and let's get it over with."
Minaya said then: "I'll do it gladly."
The girls stood up, the Cid took their hands and placed them in Minaya's.
Now Minaya is speaking to the infantes de Carrión:

> "Both you brothers, Minaya stands here before you:
> by the hand of King Alfonso,
> who has commanded me to do so,
> I give you these ladies, both
> of noble birth,
> you may take them as your wives and
> honor them lawfully."[11]

The brothers welcomed them, received them with love and joy,
and went to kiss the hands of mio Cid and his wife.
This done, they left the palace at once, and
headed toward the cathedral of Santa María.
Already in his vestments, the bishop, don Jerónimo,
stood at the church door waiting for them; he
gave them benedictions and sang the mass.
Once out of church, they take to their horses swiftly, head
for the gravel pits of Valencia. God!
how lively when they jousted at sports of arms,
mio Cid and his men!
Why, he
who was in good hour born changed horses three times!
The Cid was well satisfied with what he saw, that
the infantes de Carrión were terrific horsemen.
They returned to Valencia with the ladies, and
the wedding feasts were spread richly, throughout the great fortress.
The next day, the Cid had
seven jousting boards erected,
each of which had to be broken before
they went back in to eat lunch.

A full fifteen days the wedding feasts went on,
and about the end of that time, the nobles got ready to leave.
Mio Cid don Rodrigo, man born in a good hour,
gave away about a hundred of
        all kinds of animals:
            palfreys, mules, and swift war-horses, besides
                cloaks, furs, and other garments in abundance;
and no one could keep count of the gifts in money. Also,
        his vassals made gifts to
            whoever happened to have come,
                any guest who wanted something,
                    he was so loaded down that
                        whoever had come to the weddings,
                            returned to Castille rich.
And now the guests were leaving, saying
good-bye to Ruy Díaz, and to
all the ladies and nobles there.
They rode off, very contented with mio Cid and his vassals, and
        spoke much among themselves of how
            generously they'd been treated.
            Diego and Fernando were no less content,
                they who were the sons of count Gonzalo de Carrión.
Now the guests have left for Castille.
The Cid and his sons-in-law stay there in Valencia.
The infantes stay there nearly two years,
and the favor shown them there was beyond measure.
For the Cid and his vassals, life was pleasant indeed.
May it please St. Mary and God, the Father, in heaven
to reward the Cid, and him who arranged this marriage![12]
            The verses of this cantar are finished now.
            May the Creator and all his saints
                be with you.

THE THIRD CANTAR

The Atrocity at Corpes

112   THE CID'S LION GETS LOOSE. THE FRIGHT OF THE HEIRS
OF CARRIÓN. THE CID GENTLES THE LION. THE INFANTES ARE
ASHAMED.

> Mio Cid was living in Valencia with all his men,
> including his sons-in-law, the
> infantes de Carrión. The Cid
was lying on a bench dead asleep one day, and
a weird accident happened:
the lion snapped his leash and got out of the cage.
Great was the fear seen in midcourt,
the Campeador's men grabbed up their cloaks
and stood about the bench to protect their lord.
> One of the heirs of Carrión, Fernando González,
> found no place to hide, neither room nor tower to
> run to, and so
was in such a funk, he dived under the bench where the Cid was sleeping.
> Diego, the other infante, ran
> screaming out the door:
> "Nevermore shall I see Carrión!" and
hid behind a beam of the winepress, that scared.
Of course, his cloak and tunic got all filthy. At
> that moment, the Campeador awoke,
> "All right men, what's up, what do you want?"
> "O honored lord, the lion's given us quite a scare."

The Cid rose on one elbow, then
got to his feet.
Trailing his cloak from the shoulders, he walked straight toward the lion
The lion, when he saw him, was
   so embarrassed, he lowered his head and
     laid his muzzle on the floor.
       Mio Cid don Rodrigo
         seized him by the mane,
and led him off expertly and
put him back in the cage.
Everyone who was there was flabbergasted.
    They all returned to the main hall of the palace, the Cid
    asked for his sons-in-law—nowhere—they call their names,
      no one answers.
When finally they were located and came in, their
      faces blanched of color, you've
     never heard or seen such mockery as echoed through
     the court until
    mio Cid put an end to the jokes.
The infantes de Carrión felt themselves disgraced, and
     surely, did not take it lightly.

113   KING BÚCAR OF MOROCCO ATTACKS VALENCIA.

While the infantes were still trying to live this down,
   Moroccan armies came to besiege the town;
   on the Cuarto Plain they just settled in
   with fifty thousand of the biggest tents around.
This was the King Búcar, you'll have heard of him.

114   THE HEIRS ARE FRIGHTENED OF BATTLE. THE CID
REPROACHES THEM.

The Cid and all his men were happy indeed,
for now their spoils would increase, thanks be to God.

But it weighed heavily upon the heirs of Carrión, you know it, and
to see all those Moorish tents did their appetites no good.
      The brothers went out privately to discuss it:
      "When we married the Cid's daughters, we
      considered only the gains, not the losses. Here's
      a battle now, and no way we can get out of it.
      If we think we'll see Carrión again,
         we're only kidding ourselves,
      and the Cid's daughters will be left widows."
Muño Gustioz overheard this private conversation,
and brought their words to the Campeador:
           "Some sons-in-law you've got there,
         so daring that, now a battle's here,
       nothing they'd like better than
     to leave for Carrión.
Go console them and God help you. Let them
stay here in peace, and tell them stay out of the fight.
God'll aid us and, with you beside us, we'll win all right."
Mio Cid don Rodrigo left the room with a grin:
     "God save you, my sons, infantes de Carrión,
       in your arms[1] you hold my daughters, white as the sun!
        I love to fight, and you love Carrión, so
          just take it easy and stay here in Valencia.
I know how to handle these Moors, and'll
manage to rout them, with the help of the Lord."

115   THE ULTIMATUM FROM BÚCAR. THE CHRISTIANS
CHARGE. FERNANDO'S COWARDICE. (LACUNA AT THIS POINT IN
THE MS., SO THE FIRST FIFTY LINES [THIRTY LINES IN BLACK-
BURN'S TRANSLATION] ARE SUBSTITUTED FROM THE TEXT OF THE
CHRONICLE OF TWENTY KINGS). THE GENEROSITY OF PEDRO
BERMÚDEZ.

[They were still speaking of this when
     a message came from Búcar, demanding

that the Cid surrender Valencia.
Búcar would let him retreat peacefully, or else
he'd make the Cid pay dearly for everything he'd done.
"Go, tell Búcar,"
the Cid said to the man who'd brought the message, "tell that
son of my enemies that
within three days, I'll
give him what he's asking for."
The following day, the Cid ordered his men to arm,
and all of them rode out against the Moors. Then,
the infantes pleaded with him to
give to them the honor of first blood.
So, when the Campeador
had drawn up the lines of battle, don
Fernando, one of the heirs, dashed out ahead to
attack a Moor called Aladraf. When
the Moor caught sight of him he rode against him hard, and Femando,
without the courage to hold his ground, cut his horse around
and fled, since he did not dare to wait.
Pedro Bermúdez, who was riding close behind him,
saw what was happening, rose on to engage the Moor,
fought him and killed him.
He seized the trailing rein of the Moor's horse, rode
after the fleeing infante and said to him:
"Don Fernando, take this horse and tell them that you
killed the Moor that owned him. I'll back you up."
"Don Pedro Bermúdez," replied the infante,
"I thank you very much for those words,]
may you see the hour when I can repay you twice over."
The pair of them rode back together and
don Pedro gave his authority to the exploit
of which Fernando bragged. The tale
pleased mio Cid and all his vassals:
"If God, our Father who is in heaven wish it,
both my sons-in-law will prove good fighters in the field."

They continue talking of it, mean-
while advancing on the Moorish host
through the drums' sounding.
Many of those Christians, newly arrived in the Cid's ranks, were
astounded, not having heard them before.
The most overawed of all were Diego and Fernando, who
if they'd had their way about it,
would not have been there at all.
The Campeador shouted across:

"Hola, Pedro Bermúdez, nephew, dear fellow, please,
take good care of my sons-in-law, Diego and Fernando,
I love them both.

The Moors'll never hold this field,
God's truth!"

116   PEDRO BERMÚDEZ DECLINES TO WATCH THE HEIRS.
MINAYA AND DON JERÓNIMO BOTH ASK FOR THE ADVANCE
POSITION IN THE BATTLE.

"I tell you, Cid, in the name of all charity,
the heirs won't have me as a nursemaid,[2] not today, at least.
Let somebody else do it, I've no favor for them.
I want me and my men to be in the first wave,
you and yours hold it tight in the rear,
ready to come to my aid, should the need arise."
Minaya Álvar Fáñez came riding up:
"Ya, listen Cid, worthy Campeador,
God will earn this battle,
and you as well, who've always had his favor.
Send us to strike whatever part of their lines
seems best to you, and
every man jack of us will do his part.
With God's help and your good luck,
we'll see who gets hurt."
Mio Cid answered, "Now, just take it a little easy."

Up comes the bishop, don Jerónimo,
and heavily armed he was:
"Today I performed the mass
of the Holy Trinity for you.
I left my own country and came here to seek you out
just out of my proclivity for killing Moors. I'd like
to bring honor to my order, and to my hands, and
ask the privilege of striking the first blows. I bear
pennon and arms emblazoned with deer, and
if it please God, I should like to try them hard.
It'd please my heart, and Cid, you'd have another
reason to like me. Besides,
I'll quit you here and now if you won't grant me this."
The Cid replied then:
"I am pleased to grant your wish.
But now, here come the Moors, go try them out.
We'll watch from here and see how the abbot fights."

117   THE BISHOP SMASHES HIS WAY INTO BATTLE. THE CID
STRIKES. HE INVADES THE MOORISH CAMP.

The bishop don Jerónimo began his charge
and it carried him all the way to the end of their camp.
With good luck and God's grace, he killed two Moors with the first blows.
His lance snapped, and he set hand to his sword and
tried that out on them, God, how that bishop fought!
Two he killed with the lance and five with the sword.
Great numbers of Moors surrounded him,
dealt him great blows, but
could not break through the armor.
The man born in a good hour kept his eye on him, braced
his shield in position and lowered his lance, set
spurs to his swift-pacing horse Babieca and
drove into the press with heart and soul.
Breaking through the first few ranks,

the Campeador unseated seven and killed four.
As it pleased God, the rout was well begun.
        The Cid and his men hurled themselves recklessly
                into the pursuit. Everywhere
                    tent ropes snapped,
                        stakes were uprooted,
tent poles crashed to earth with the handsome tents.
The Cid's men whipped Búcar's troops and chased them
                out of their own camp.

118   THE CHRISTIANS PRESS THE ENEMY CLOSELY. THE CID
OVERTAKES AND KILLS BÚCAR. HE CAPTURES THE SWORD
"TIZÓN."

They drove them away from the tents
        and took up the pursuit.
            Here and there, you'd see
an arm hacked off, still wrapped in its coat of mail,
                heads still wearing helmets rolled on the earth,
                    riderless horses running in all directions. The chase
            went on for a full seven miles. The Cid
overtook King Búcar, called out:
"Turn around there, Búcar, you've
come all the way from overseas, now
you must settle things with the Cid of the long beard. We
must kiss one another and swear peace."
            "Damn all such friendship, you've
        got that sword in your hand coming at top speed,
and I'd like to bet you intend to try it against me.
                No thanks.
If my horse doesn't stumble, you'll never get close enough to fight,
unless you want to follow me into the sea."
        The Cid replied, "That just won't be the case, watch."
Now, Búcar had a good horse that could cover ground,
            but the Cid's Babieca was closing on him.

Some seventeen feet from the surf line, the Cid caught up with Búcar,
raised the sword Colada and dealt him a great stroke, clove
the jewels from his helmet, drove through the helmet,
                    splitting him down to the crotch.
        He'd killed Búcar, the king from across the sea, and won
the sword Tizón, worth a thousand marks of gold.
Mio Cid had won a great and marvelous battle,
                    to his honor,
        and all those who are with him that day
                    have gained honor.

119   THE CAMPEADOR'S MEN RETURN FROM THE CHASE. THE
CID IS SATISFIED WITH HIS SONS-IN-LAW; THEY ARE ASHAMED.
THE SPOILS OF THE VICTORY.

        They were returning from the pursuit with their prizes,
stripping the field thoroughly as they came, naturally.
They arrive at the tents with mio Cid Ruy Díaz,
                    the famous Campeador. He
rode swiftly across the fields strewn with the slaughtered, carrying
                    two swords, Tizón and Colada,
                    both of which he prized highly,
hood and helmet back, face bare, his cloth cap somewhat wrinkled,
                    but still on his hair. His
                    vassals are coming in from all directions:
                    mio Cid raised his eyes and held them fast on
        a sight that pleased his heart: coming in were
the sons of count Gonzalo, the brothers Diego and Fernando.
The Cid was elated and smiled broadly:
"You're back, my sons-in-law, both of you my own true sons!
        I see you've enjoyed fighting, and all Carrión
            shall know of it, and how we've beaten Búcar.
                As I put my trust in God and all
                his saints, I reckon we'll ride off
                well rewarded for this victory."

At this point, Minaya Álvar Fáñez rode up, his
buckler hung from his neck battered and dented by swords
and thrusts of lances turned aside; those
>who had dealt the blows
>>had not had the profit from them. Blood
>>was still streaming from his elbow, he'd
>>>killed over twenty Moors.
>>"Thanks be to God in heaven and to you, Cid! You've
>>killed Búcar, and the field is ours!
>>All this stuff lying around is yours and ours. And here
your sons-in-law have been tried and proved themselves,
and are surfeited with battling Moors in the field."
Said the Cid,
>>>"I'm pleased with the performance.
>>>If they were good today, in time
>>>they'll be irreplaceable."
>>>>The Cid had spoken sincerely, but
>>>>the brothers took it as mockery.
All the loot
was carted into Valencia.
The Cid is merry and
so are all his vassals, for each share was worth
six hundred silver marks. The Cid's sons-in-law,
>>>when they had taken their portions,
they put their share from the victory away carefully, and figured
they'd never lack for money again for the rest of their lives.
>>The Valencianos were abundantly provided for,
>>lots of good food, fine furs, and rich clothing.
>>Mio Cid and his vassals,
>>all were rejoicing.

120   THE CID IS SATISFIED WITH THE VICTORY AND WITH
HIS SONS-IN-LAW (REPETITION).

It was a great day in the Campeador's court, after this

battle was won and King Búcar killed. The Cid
      lifted his hand and tugged his beard:
      "Thanks be to Christ, king of this world, now,
      I've seen what I longed to see, both
      my sons-in-law have fought in the field beside me.
      A worthy account of them will go to Carrión, how
      they've won honor for themselves and helped us greatly."

121   THE ALLOTTING OF THE BOOTY.

The spoils everyone
had won were enormous,
portions they added to gains they'd already taken.
Mio Cid, born in a good hour, ordered that all
take the shares that were theirs by right from this battle they'd won,
         but for God's sake, not
      to forget his twenty percent.
      Which they don't, no disagreement.
Six hundred horses fell to the Cid's fifth, and
so many beasts of burden and big camels that
         no one could keep count of them.

122   AT THE CULMINATION OF HIS GLORY, THE CID CON-
TEMPLATES TAKING MOROCCO. THE INFANTES LIVE RICHLY AND
IN HONOR IN THE CID'S COURT.

The Campeador had earned all these prizes.
      "Thanks be to God who is Lord of this world!
      Not too long ago I was poor, and now am rich,
         have wealth and lands, and gold and honor, I
         have the infantes de Carrión as sons-in-law.
            With God's grace, I win my battles. Moors
            and Christians both go in fear of me. Maybe
         in that Morocco full of mosques far off they fear
I'll fall upon them suddenly some dark night.

But no, I'll stay here in Valencia and not go
looking for a fight.
They can send their tribute money here to me, or
to whomever I choose, if God helps me so."
                    In Valencia were great celebrations
                    among all the Cid's companions in
                honor of this victory they'd won in a stiff fight.
Both sons-in-law were elated, be-
tween them they were entitled to five thousand marks and
thought of themselves as rich men, these infantes de Carrión.
They joined the others at court. The
bishop don Jerónimo was there with the Cid, and too,
good Álvar Fáñez, that fighting knight,
                        and many others whom
            the Campeador had brought up in his own home. When
the heirs entered, Minaya
received them in the Cid's name:
"So come on in, kinsmen, we're honored by your being here."
            That they had come pleased the Campeador:
                My sons-in-law, here is my wife,
                    and my daughters, doña Elvira and doña Sol, let them
hold you tight and do your pleasure with all their hearts!
Thanks be to Mary, mother of our Lord God, you shall
                have gained honor from this marriage, and
                    the fame of your name will travel
                        to the lands of Carrión!"

123   THE VANITY OF THE INFANTES. THE JOKES OF WHICH
THEY ARE THE BUTT.

At these words, Fernando spoke:
                    "I thank the Lord and thank you,
honored Cid, that
we've riches so great that no one can count them.
Because of you we have honor,

we have fought for you, we've beaten Moors in the field, we've
killed King Búcar, that bastard. Our
own estate is assured, you can turn
your attention to other matters."
        The Cid's vassals sat there smiling:
        some had fought hardily, some
        had been forward in the pursuit,
but no one had seen Diego and Fernando
anywhere.
Because these jokes floating around day and night
scored so deeply on them, the
infantes conceived together a devilish plan. They
went outside, indeed they were brothers, and
what they spoke of, let us have no part of it:
        "We've been here too long, that's for sure, let's
        start back to Carrión. The
      wealth we have by now is great, overwhelming even, we
could not manage to spend it for the rest of our lives.

124   THE INFANTES DECIDE TO DISHONOR THE CID'S DAUGH-
TERS. THEY ASK THE CID IF THEY CAN TAKE THEIR WIVES TO
CARRIÓN. THE CID CONSENTS. THE WEDDING CLOTHES HE GIVES
TO HIS DAUGHTERS. THE INFANTES GET READY TO LEAVE. THE
DAUGHTERS TAKE LEAVE OF THEIR FATHER.

—"Let us ask the Cid Campeador
      for our wives, we'll tell him
         we're taking them to Carrión
           to show them what great lands their
             inheritances are. We'll
get them out of Valencia, out of the Cid's power, and later,
on the road, we'll do what we like with them,
before anyone drags out that lion story again.
Our family is that of the counts of Carrión!
We'll take all these riches with us, and besides

we'll dishonor the daughters of the Campeador."
    —"We'll be wealthy forever with the riches we have now,
    we can marry the daughters of kings or emperors, for we're
    of the family of the counts of Carrión.
    Thus we'll punish the Cid's daughters before
    they bring up that lion business again."
Having come to the decision, they
went back into the court,
and requested the court be silent:
                "May the Creator bless you, Cid Campeador!
        If it pleases the doña Jimena, and you first of all, and
        Minaya Álvar Fáñez, and the rest of those here present,
        give us our wives, duly married under blessing, to
        take them to our lands in Carrión, that
        they may, in fact, have the lands we gave them at the wedding
        for their honor. Your
        daughters will see what we possess, and
        our sons-to-be will have the division of it."
Mio Cid el Campeador, suspecting no harm, replied:
"I give you my daughters and other treasure of mine. You
        have given them marriage villas in Carrión, I
            wish to add three thousand marks to the marriage gifts, and
give you mules and palfreys, well grown and trained, strong and
        fast-running war-horses to walk at your right hand,
            and garments woven of silk and gold brocade. I shall
                give you the two swords,
                    Colada and Tizón,
I've won them as a man ought to, you should know.
I give you my daughters, so you are both my sons, and you're
taking away the warp and woof of my heart in so doing. Let them know
        in what richness I send off my sons-in-law, let them
            know in Galicia, in Castille, and in León.
                Look after my daughters, your wives, if you
                    treat them well, I'll see you're well rewarded."
The infantes de Carrión have agreed and given their word, re-

ceived the Cid's daughters. Now they begin
to accept the gifts the Cid had commanded for them.
When they have collected all the gifts they could want, the
infantes de Carrión ordered everything packed up.
       Great was the commotion in Valencia the great, all
          taking arms and leaping on horseback to
            send the Cid's daughters off
              to Carrión. They
          are ready to ride, are taking leave. Both
        sisters, doña Elvira and doña Sol,
      knelt before Cid Campeador:
"God be your assistance, father, and may we
beg a favor of you?
Lady and lord, on our knees before you, our father who sired us and
our mother who bore us: you send us off now to Carrión, and we
must obey whatever you say, we beg,
both of us, your blessings, and please write?"
      Mio Cid hugged and kissed them both.

125   JIMENA SAYS GOOD-BYE TO HER DAUGHTERS. THE CID
RIDES OUT TO SEE THE TRAVELERS OFF. BAD OMENS OCCUR.

He embraced them, their mother hugged them twice over:
"Go, my daughters, the Creator watch over you from now on!
You have our blessings, both from me and your father. Now
go be heiresses in Carrión. I'm
sure you've made good marriages, my dears."
They kissed their father's and mother's hands, both parents
blessed them and gave them their love.
      Mio Cid and the others started to ride off, all
         decked out in fine armor, and the horses also bespangled.
           Then the infantes rode out
              from Valencia, that shining city, after
taking leave of the ladies-in-waiting and all their companions.

Mio Cid and his men rode on cheerfully
    through the orchards around Valencia,
        horsing around and sporting about with their arms.
        Though, he who was born in a good hour
          looked at omens and saw
that these marriages would not escape some stain.
But now is hardly the time for him to regret it,
both of the girls are married.

126   THE CID SENDS FELÍX MUÑOZ ALONG WITH HIS DAUGH-
TERS. THE LAST FAREWELL. THE TRAIN ARRIVES AT MOLINA.
ABENGALBÓN ACCOMPANIES THEM AS FAR AS MEDINACELI. THE
HEIRS ARE THINKING ABOUT KILLING ABENGALBÓN.

        "All right, Muñoz, where are you?
        Félix, nephew, dearest cousin to both my daughters! I
        order you to go with them
          all the way to Carrión. You'll
        inspect the lands given them in marriage, come
          back and report to me."
"I'll do that gladly," said Félix Muñoz.
Then Minaya Álvar Fáñez stopped before mio Cid:
        "Let's get on back to Valencia, Cid. If it
        please God, our Father and Creator, someday
          we'll go to see them in Carrión and those lands."
"Doña Elvira and doña Sol, we commend you to God,
let whatever you do make us proud of you."
        The sons-in-law answered for them:
        "May God will it so."
        At taking leave, the sorrow was immense. The
        father and his daughters wept openly, as also did
        the knights of the Campeador.
        "Now listen, Félix Muñoz, my nephew, go
        by way of Molina and spend the night there.

> Say hello to my friend Abengalbón for me, have him
> receive my sons-in-law with his best hospitality, tell him
> I'm sending my daughters to Carrión, that he should
> serve their pleasure, whatever they need, and
> for love of me, escort them as far as Medinaceli.
> Anything he does for them, I shall reward him well."
>> Their parting was like pulling a fingernail from the flesh.

The man who was in good hour born started
back toward Valencia. The infantes de Carrión
continued forward, made their camp overnight at
Santa María de Albarracín.

> The following day, they whip leather until
>> they come to Molina, whose lord is Abengalbón.

When the Moor knew who they were, it pleased his heart, he
rode out to greet them in great excitement. God! how
well he served them in whatever pleased them.
The next morning he rode off with them
along with two hundred knights he'd ordered as escort.

> They crossed the high wooded country known as the
>> Luzón Range, across the Arbujuelo Valley and
>>> arrived at the Jalón, set up camp at a place
>>>> called Ansarera.

The Moor presented his gifts to the Cid's daughters,
and fine horses to each one of the heirs.
All this the Moor did out of love for el Cid Campeador.
When they saw the wealth of things the Moor had brought, these two brothers
> plotted treachery against him:
>> "Since we're already planning to desert
>>> the Cid's daughters, we might as well
>>>> murder this Moor Abengalbón if possible, and
>>>>> whatever wealth he has on him we can have for ourselves.

We can keep it as safe as our own in Carrión, and
el Cid Campeador will never have rights over us for it."
While the infantes de Carrión were hatching this scheme, it seems
that a Moor who understood Castillian overheard them and

kept it no secret, you know,
>   told Abengalbón:
>   "Master, my lord, beware of these two,
>   for I've heard them plotting to kill you,
>   these heirs of Carrión."

127   ABENGALBÓN LEAVES THE PARTY, THREATENING THE
INFANTES.

The Moor Abengalbón was one
>   tough son-of-a-gun, came
riding up to confront the brothers, his two hundred knights with him,
arms at ready: what the Moor said to the heirs was far from cheerful.
>   "If it were not for the great
>   respect I have for
>   mio Cid, el de Bivar, I'd
give it to you so hard, the blows would ring around the world!
I'd return his daughters to the loyal Campeador, and you'd
never see Carrión again, and that's for sure!

128   THE MOOR GOES BACK TO MOLINA, FORESEEING THAT
MISFORTUNES ARE ABOUT TO OCCUR TO THE CID'S DAUGHTERS.
THE TRAVELERS COME INTO CASTILLE. THEY SLEEP IN THE WOOD
OF CORPES. IN THE MORNING THE INFANTES STAY ALONE WITH
THEIR WIVES AND GET READY TO BEAT THEM UP. THE HOPELESS
BEGGING OF DOÑA SOL. THE HEIRS' CRUELTY.

"Infantes de Carrión indeed! Say something! What have I done to you?
I do you a service in all good faith, and
what are you up to? You're plotting my death. I'm not
going another step with such butchers.
>   Your permission, doña Elvira and doña Sol, I'm leaving. I've
>   only contempt for the fame of the heirs of Carrión.
>   May God, the lord of this world, grant that
>   the Cid never regret your marriages!"

This said, the Moor turned back
and crossed the river Jalón, still with his arms at ready. Like
a man with a brain in his head, he returned to Molina.
　　　　　　The infantes moved out from Ansarera,
　　　　　　　　traveling day and night; they passed
　　　　　　　　　Atienza on their left, a fort on
a very strong hill, then crossed the Sierra de Miedes,
hurried through the Montes Claros; hitting the spurs
they leave Griza to their left, the town Álamos settled, and there
the caves where he kept Elpha[3] captive, and still further on to where
　　　　　　San Esteban de Gormaz lay to their right.
　　　　　　The infantes entered the oak grove at Corpes,
　　　　　　　　high mountains, the trees' branches scrape
　　　　　　　　　the clouds, wild beasts roam. They found
a flower-filled clearing with a clear-running spring and
ordered the tent set up.
With as many as were with them, there they spent the night; they
took their young wives in their arms
and faked it, love's proof,[4] yet
the sunrise will show an accomplished brutality!
　　　　　　In the morning, they had the animals loaded with all the treasure,
　　　　　　　had the tents struck where they had spent the night, all
　　　　　　　their household people have ridden ahead as ordered.
　　　　　　The infantes de Carrión make sure
　　　　　　　neither the knights or their wives remain,
　　　　　　　no one except doña Elvira and doña Sol,
　　　　　　　　their own wives, with whom they
　　　　　　　　　wish to play as they will, for their own pleasure.
Everyone else has gone ahead, these four are left alone;
the heirs of Carrión turn to the atrocity they've planned:
　　　　　　"Doña Elvira and doña Sol, now we're alone
　　　　　　　here in these savage mountains,
it's we who are going to have the laugh today, you'd better believe it.

We're going off and we're going to leave you here, you'll never
                    see your lands in Carrión.
The news'll get back to the Campeador, and we'll be
                    avenged for that business about the lion."
Then they tore the cloaks and tunics off the girls,
leaving them only their chemises and underclothes.
The sons of bitches are wearing spurs and in their hands
they've got great, heavy saddle cinches. When
the ladies saw this, doña Sol spoke out:
"By God, we ask you, *we* ask you, don Diego and don Fernando!
you've got two good strong swords there, very sharp,
                  one called Colada and the other Tizón.
         Behead us at least and martyr us. Moors and
Christians alike will repudiate the deed and any reason for it,
for whatever we may deserve, it's not this. Do not commit
             such a villainous deed upon us. You'll only
                vilify yourselves if you whip us, and they'll
have you up in a straight encounter, or before the court."
                  The girls' pleading does them no good, the heirs
                  begin to work them over with the leather cinches,
                  the straps slithering down; with their spurs, they
                  rake them painfully, the spurs are sharp, they
                  tear the shirts and flesh of both girls, the blood
                  runs brightly over the silken shifts, God! They
                  feel it in their very hearts! Please, God, let
                  the Cid Campeador appear now, what a
                  scene that would be!
But they beat them senseless,
blood all over their shirts and silk underclothes;
both men vying to see which of them can whip the harder;
                  finally they get tired. Doña
                  Elvira and doña Sol can
                  no longer speak.

The heirs leave them for dead in the forest of Corpes.

129   THE INFANTES ABANDON THEIR WIVES (*PARALLEL PASSAGE*).

They cart off the cloaks and ermine furs, leaving
the girls half-naked and passed out, in their silken shifts and shirts,
leaving them to the birds on the mountain and the wild beasts.
Realize, they thought them dead, showing no signs of life.
O, if the Cid Ruy Díaz had come upon them in that hour!

130   THE INFANTES BOAST OF THEIR COWARDICE.

Neither girl moves to help the other, so
the infantes de Carrión leave them there, thinking them dead.
Going on through the mountains, they
congratulate themselves:
                    "Well, we got rid of those bitches and have
                    avenged our marriages.
If we hadn't been importuned, we wouldn't have taken them as whores.
                    They were unworthy to be our lawful wives.
        And so that humiliation with the lion will be avenged."

131   FÉLIX MUÑOZ SUSPECTS THE INFANTES. HE TURNS
BACK LOOKING FOR THE CID'S DAUGHTERS. HE REVIVES THEM
AND TAKES THEM ON HIS HORSE BACK TO SAN ESTEBAN DE
GORMAZ. NEWS OF THEIR DISHONOR REACHES THE CID. MINAYA
GOES TO SAN ESTEBAN TO COLLECT THE GIRLS. THE MEETING
BETWEEN MINAYA AND HIS COUSINS.

                    So the heirs of Carrión went on boasting. But let me
                    tell you now about Félix Muñoz, the Cid's nephew. They
                had ordered him to ride onward, but he
        was not very happy about it.

Riding along the path, very doubtful in his heart, he
   swung off the road apart from the rest and hid
      in a thick wooded section of the mountain, to
         watch until his cousins rode by, or to see
            what the heirs of Carriōn had done. He
saw them coming along and overheard snatches of their talk; they
neither saw him, nor knew he could hear what they were saying;
if they'd seen him, he would not have escaped death, you know it.
The infantes gallop past, and Félix Muñoz turned back on the trail
        and found his cousins half-dead. Crying
"Cousins, cousins!" he jumped down off his horse,
       tethered it, and ran to them:
           "O cousins, O my cousins, doña Elvira, doña Sol!
The infantes de Carrión have shown vile proof of their natures, may God
           give them what's coming to them!"
He stayed there, trying to bring them to;
they were still so dazed, he
couldn't get them to say anything. His
heartstrings were bursting, yelling:
           "Cousins, cousins, Elvira, Sol, for
             God's love, wake up! Wake up
          while it's still light,
        before night gets here and
      wild animals come and eat us in these mountains!"
    Doña Elvira and doña Sol are coming to. They open their
eyes and see Félix Muñoz:
"Cousins, please, God's love, take strength, push yourselves a little,
    when the heirs find I'm missing, they'll come looking, and
       if God doesn't help us, all of us will die here."
      Doña Sol spoke painfully:
        "God's love, cousin, if
        our father the Campeador deserves your grace,
        give us a little water."
          Félix Muñoz took his hat, a brand

new one from Valencia, got some
water in it,
brought it to his cousins.
Both were badly beaten and could use it. He
pleaded with them, till both at least were sitting upright, went on
comforting them, giving them heart, until they were somewhat recovered,
put both of them upon his horse's back quickly as he could, covered
them both with his cloak, took hold of the horse's reins
and started out.
Alone,
the three of them,
through the oak forest of Corpes;
through the night and until the next day, they
went out from among the mountains.
They have gotten as far as
the waters of the Duero.
And he leaves the girls at the Tower of doña Urraca.[5]
At Esteban,
Félix Muñoz came across Diego Téllez, Álvar Fáñez's man.
When Diego Téllez heard the story, he was sore as hell, he
rounded up some animals,
threw on some good clothes,
and went out to receive doña Elvira and doña Sol, brought them
back to San Esteban and put them up as best he could, with
every respect and attention.
The people of Esteban, always civil folk, were
outraged,
hearing of this outrage, and
brought gifts of grain, meat, and wine to the Cid's daughters.
They stayed in that town
until they were all healed.
Meanwhile the infantes de Carrión continued to boast,
and what they'd done
became known throughout all those lands. King Alfonso
was deeply shocked. And those messages reached finally

the great city of Valencia.

When they told the news to mio Cid Campeador he sat for a
                        long time in thought,
                        raised his hand
                        and tugged at the beard:
        "Thanks be to Christ who is lord of this world, when
        the heirs of Carrión have done me any such honor.
        I swear by this beard that none has ever set hand to,
        the infantes won't get away with this.
                As for my daughters,
                        I'll marry them well yet!"
It weighed hard on mio Cid, and
his depression ran through the whole court.
Álvar Fáñez, especially, was touched, heart and soul.
                Minaya saddled up, so did Pedro Bermúdez,
                and Martín Antolínez, that worthy man of Burgos,
along with two hundred knights that the Cid sent with them.
                        He gave them strict orders to travel day and night,
                        and bring his daughters back to Valencia.
They do not hesitate
        to obey their lord's command,
                but ride quickly and keep going day and night, until
they came to Gormaz, a very strong castle, and there, truly,
they did put up for one night.
                        The news arrived at San Esteban that
                        Minaya is coming for his cousins.
The men of San Esteban, and worthy men they are, come
        out to welcome Minaya and all his company, and
that night present Minaya with great offerings of food and wine.[6]
                He did not wish to accept them, but thanked them warmly:
        "For the honor that you do us in this misfortune, men of Esteban,
                thank you, for you know how to act like men.
Mio Cid Campeador, off there in Valencia, thanks you deeply,
        as I do standing here before you.
May God in heaven see that you're well rewarded!"

Everyone thanks Minaya
and all are pleased with him. Then
all of them go home to get a night's rest.
Minaya heads
straight in to where his cousins are staying.
When doña Elvira and doña Sol lay eyes on him, they cry:
"We couldn't be happier to see you than if you were God himself,
and you may thank him that we're alive at all. When
there's more time back in Valencia, we'll tell you the whole miserable story."

132   MINAYA AND HIS COUSINS LEAVE SAN ESTEBAN. EL CID
RIDES OUT TO WELCOME THEM.

The girls broke into tears, as did Álvar Fáñez,
and Pedro Bermúdez spoke to them for a while:
"Doña Elvira and doña Sol, now
don't do that, you've no more cares, you're safe and sound,
nothing else to worry about.
So you've lost good marriages, don't worry,
you'll find better ones maybe,
and we'll see the day we can avenge you yet!"
And they spent the night there
and enjoyed themselves immensely.
The next morning they got ready to ride; the
population of San Esteban went out with them
escorting them as far as Rio d'amor,
keeping them company. There they
said good-bye to the travelers and
turned back; Minaya
and the ladies con-
tinued on their way.

They passed through Alcoceba, leaving Gormaz
                    behind them on their right,
through the town called Vadorrey and stopped for the night in the
                    town of Berlanga.
They got going again in the morning and went
                    as far as Medinaceli
                    before they quit for the day.
          From Medinaceli to Molina,
          they made the trip in a single day, and
      Abengalbón the Moor, profoundly pleased,
came out to welcome them gladly,
gave them a palatial meal for the Cid's sake.
The next morning they headed straight for Valencia.
Word of their arrival came to the man
          born in a good hour. He saddled quickly
          and rode out to receive them, waving
                    his weapons about festively, showing his pleasure.
Mio Cid rode up to embrace his daughters, kissed them both, and
                    a big smile crossed his face:
                    "You're here, my daughters? God
          keep you from further harm!
      I took it,
your marriages, I mean, having no choice in the matter, dared
          say nothing. May it please God in heaven,
          I see you better married than that hereafter,
                    and may He grant me vengeance against
                    my sons-in-law!"
The daughters kissed their father's hands.
Playing at weapons, the company entered the city, where Jimena
                    rejoiced greatly at seeing her daughters.
The man born in a good hour had no intention of wasting time;

he called in his men to have a private talk with them,
and prepared to send a petition to King Alfonso in Castille.

133   THE CID SENDS MUÑO GUSTIOZ TO BEG THE KING'S
JUSTICE. MUÑO FINDS THE KING IN SAHAGÚN AND EXPLAINS HIS
MESSAGE. THE KING PROMISES COMPENSATION.

"Are you there, Muño Gustioz, my excellent vassal?
A good day I took you into my court to raise!
You'll take a message to Castille, to King Alfonso,
kiss his hand for me, in token that he
is my true lord, and I remain his vassal—this
dishonor that they've done me, these infantes de Carrión,
I want it to grieve the king as deeply as it does me,
and that's heart and soul.
It was he who gave my daughters in marriage, I'd
nothing to say about it.
Since they've been dishonored and left, any
disgrace to us, any affront to us in this matter, great or small,
is his as well.
They've taken from me
wealth unmeasured as well, and that
I have to count as a further dishonor.
Just get them into court for me,
any meeting or assembly will do.[7]
And I want my rights from them,
these infantes de Carrión,
for great is the rancor I carry in my heart."
Muño Gustioz rode off quickly, with
two knights at his disposal, and
a number of squires from his own household. They
left Valencia riding as hard as they could,
and gave themselves no rest day or night.
They ran down King Alfonso in Sahagún.

King he is of Castille, king of León and Asturias, of the
city of Oviedo and as far as Santiago, he is
lord of all that, the
    counts of Galicia serve him as their lord.
    As soon as Muño Gustioz dismounted, he
made grateful greeting to the saints of that place, offered
a prayer to the Creator, rose, and headed for the palace
where the court was.
   With him were the two knights who served him as their lord.
    Thus, they came into midcourt, the king
    saw them, recognized Muño Gustioz,
    rose and received them graciously. That same
Muño Gustioz fell to his knees before King Alfonso and kissed his feet:
"Your mercy, O King,
    the great kingdoms that call you lord! The
Campeador kisses your feet and hands; you are his lord, and he
    your faithful vassal.
You married his daughters to the heirs of Carrión; the
match was exalted because of your interest in it, well,
   you know how much honor the marriage has done us, how
    the infantes de Carrión have laid insult on us.
They whipped the Cid's daughters, whipped and stripped them bare, left them
dishonored, abandoned them to the mercy of wild beasts and mountain birds,
in the oak grove of Corpes.
He has the girls back in Valencia now.
As vassal to his lord, the Cid Campeador now kisses your hands, begs
you bring them to confrontation in court or assembly.
He knows he's been gravely insulted, but
   the insult to you is worse;
    as you are wise,
let it weigh upon you equally, O King, and let the Cid
    have satisfaction from the heirs of Carrión."
    The king was silent for a long hour,
    sat and meditated:

"Tell you the truth about this, it's
heavy on my heart. You
say the truth, Muño Gustioz, it was I
married his daughters to the infantes.
I did it for his best interest, I did it to his advantage. Today,
I sure wish it hadn't happened, to me or the Cid either, his grief is mine.
Let the Creator help me, I'll see that he gets justice!
I didn't think I'd have to do it this time of year, but,
I'll send the heralds throughout my kingdom to call
a full court to meet in Toledo. All
counts and noblemen are to attend, and I
shall order the infantes de Carrión specifically
to come there and give satisfaction
to mio Cid el Campeador.
If I can prevent it, he won't be left with a grievance for long, believe it.

134   THE KING CONVOKES COURT IN TOLEDO.

"Tell the Campeador,
he who was born in a good hour,
to be ready with his vassals seven
weeks from now,
ready to come to Toledo, those are the terms.
I call this court out of friendship for mio Cid Campeador.
Give my best to everyone, tell them 'relax,'
there still may be some honor for them from this catastrophe."
Muño Gustioz took his leave and
returned to the Cid. Alfonso
of Castille, as good as his word, hesi-
tates not a moment, sends his letters out throughout León,
to Santiago, to the Portuguese, the Galicians, and to Carrión,
and throughout Castille, telling everybody and everyone
that the court would be in session in Toledo

seven weeks hence,
and that their honored king
said that they should be there.
Anybody that didn't come would no longer be considered his vassal.
Through all his lands the heralds rode, thinking
and rightly so, that no one would fail to do
what the king had ordered.

135   THOSE OF CARRIÓN BEG IN VAIN THAT THE KING
DESIST FROM HOLDING THE COURT. THE CID ARRIVES LAST OF
ALL. THE KING GOES OUT TO MEET HIM.

Already, the infantes de Carrión
are pacing about, very worried
that the king is convening a court in Toledo, afraid that
mio Cid Campeador will be there.
They ask advice of relatives, end up by
begging the king to excuse them from this court.
"God help me, I will not!" said the king,
"for Cid Campeador will be there, and you
must give him satisfaction for
the grievance he has against you.
Anyone who does not wish to make it, or will not come to my court,
let him leave my kingdom, I'll have nothing to do with him."
The heirs of Carrión saw there was no way to get out of it.
Again they took counsel with all their relatives,
chief among whom in this business was count
don García, the Cid's enemy, who
took every opportunity to do him harm;
he was to be the infantes' chief advisor.
The appointed time was near, people were
beginning to assemble.
Among the first to arrive

were good King Alfonso, count don Enrique, and count don Ramón—
he was father of the good emperor—count don Fruela, and count don Birbón.
Gathered from throughout the kingdom were men most learned in law,
and the best there were from all over Castille.

    There came also the count don García, old Pruneface of Grañón,
        and Álvar Díaz who commanded Oca, and
          Asur González,
          and Gonzalo Ansúrez, you could bet on that,
          along with Diego and Fernando and
a great crowd with them which they brought along to the court,
        hoping to attack mio Cid Campeador.

          People have assembled from every direction, though
          the man in a good hour born had not arrived, and
          his delay is starting to annoy the king.
On the fifth day, mio Cid el Campeador came,
        sending Álvar Fáñez ahead
          to kiss the hands of the king, his lord, and to
          say to expect him by nightfall.
Happy to hear it, the king mounted his horse,
rode out with an impressive retinue to
receive the Campeador.
The Cid with his men are coming ready for anything,
a goodly company, worthy of such a lord.

        When he came in sight of the good king, the
          Campeador threw himself to the ground, he
           wanted to humble himself to honor his lord; the
           king saw him and protested at once:
"By Sant Isidro, I'll have none of that today! Get
back on your horse, Cid, unless
you wish to displease me. We must
greet one another equally, heart and soul. The
trouble you've had grieves my heart as well.
May God grant today you honor the court by your presence!"

          "Amen to that," replied the Cid, good Campeador; he
           kissed the king's hand and then his mouth.

"At the sight of you, my lord, I give thanks to God. My
respects to you, to the count Ramón, count don Enrique,
and as many others as are with you.
God save you most, my lord,
and all our friends. Doña Jimena,
my wife, that gentle lady,
and both my daughters kiss your hands, my lord, and beg
that you take to heart that which has afflicted us."
The king replied, "I do, so help me God!"

136   THE CID DOES NOT ENTER TOLEDO, BUT HOLDS HIS
VIGIL IN SAN SERVANDO.

The king starts back toward Toledo,
but the Cid prefers that night
not to cross the Tagus:
"A favor, ya, King, and may the Creator keep you!
Return if you will to the city, I and my men
will stay at San Serván. The
rest of my company will join me there tonight. I'll
hold vigil in that holy place, enter
the city tomorrow morning and shall
be at the court before I've broken fast."
The king replied, "I am pleased it be so."
The king returns to the city of Toledo; mio
Cid goes back to lodge at San Serván; there
he had candles lit and set on the altar, was
happy to keep vigil in that holy place; the night
was spent in lonely prayer and private communion.
When morning came,
Minaya and the other good fellows with him
were waiting and ready.

137   IN SAN SERVÁN, THE CID'S PREPARATIONS TO ATTEND
THE COURT. THE CID GOES TO TOLEDO, HIS ENTRANCE AT THE

COURT. THE KING OFFERS HIM A SEAT ON THE BENCH BESIDE
HIM. THE CID REFUSES. THE KING OPENS THE SESSION. HE PRO-
CLAIMS PEACE BETWEEN THE LITIGANTS. THE CID PRESENTS HIS
DEMAND. HE CLAIMS RESTITUTION OF COLADA AND TIZÓN. THE
INFANTES DE CARRIÓN GIVE UP THE SWORDS. THE CID PRESENTS
THEM TO PEDRO BERMÚDEZ AND MARTIN ANTOLÍNEZ. THE CID'S
SECOND DEMAND, HIS DAUGHTERS' DOWRY. THE INFANTES
ENCOUNTER SOME DIFFICULTY IN GETTING UP THE MONEY.

In the hours before dawn, they
         said matins and prime, mass was out
           before the sun was up, and
           they'd left good-sized offerings.
"You, Minaya Álvar Fáñez,
you'll come with me,
and bishop don Jerónimo, Pedro Bermúdez, Muño Gustioz,
and Martín Antolínez our worthy man of Burgos,
and Álvar Álvarez, Álvar Salvadórez, Martín Muñoz, bless the hour you
were born, and my nephew, Félix Muñoz;
        Mal Anda will go with me,
           he's learned in law,
and Galindo García, that good fighter from Aragón.
        Including these, round out the number to
         a hundred of the best knights I have.
So you can bear the weight of the armor, wear your padded shirts
underneath your coats of mail, white as the sun,
and over the mail wear furs and ermines, and
        fasten them tightly so the weapons will not be seen,
         under the mantles have your sweet sharp swords; thus
          I intend to go to the court to demand my rights
          and speak my piece. If
the infantes de Carrión come looking for anything else, I've
nothing to worry about, with such a hundred about me."
        All answered,

"That's how we'd like it too."
And all armored up as he had indicated.
Nor did the Cid waste any time. He pulled
breeches of fine cloth on over his legs,
pulled on boots of fine worked leather;
next, a shirt of soft silk, white as the sun,
with gold and silver fastenings down the front
and fitted tight at the cuffs as he had ordered;
over that, a tunic brocaded with gold, so that
it sparkled everyplace; over these
the cloak of crimson leather with golden stripes
which the Cid always wore.
Over his head he drew a fine linen hood, embroidered with gold,
so that no one would get a chance to insult him by pulling his hair,
and took the precaution also of tying his long beard back
with a cord, for the same reason,
he wished to keep his person from insult.
Over all he threw a mantle of great value,
anyone who'd seen him wear it
had admired it.
With those hundred knights he'd
ordered to make ready, he
mounted quickly and rode out from San Serván.
Thus, ready for anything, mio Cid Campeador went to the court.
Though he dismounted with a certain relish at the outer door,
mio Cid and his men entered with due caution;
he walked to midcourt with his hundred about him.
When they saw him come in,
the man born in a good hour,
King Alfonso rose, as did count
don Enrique and count don Ramón,
and then the others there present:
with great honor they welcomed
el mio Cid Campeador.

The Pruneface of Grañón did not wish to rise, nor
did any of the Carrión faction. The king
took the Cid by the hands:
> "Come here and sit with me, Campeador,
> on this bench which you gave me as a gift;
> whomever it may displease, you are better than we."

Then he, who had taken Valencia, thanked him heartily:
> "But sit on your bench as our lord and king;
> I'll just stay here with my men."

The Cid's preference was deeply pleasing to the king. The
Campeador sat down on a bench of turned wood, and
his hundred guards seated themselves about him.
> Everyone in the court is gazing in wonder at mio Cid,
> his long beard tied back with a cord, the
> way he looked was manly in every sense of the word. The
> infantes de Carrión cannot raise their eyes for shame.

Then good King Alfonso stood up:
> "Hear me, my vassals, and
> may the Lord protect you!

Since I've been king, I've held no more than two courts: one was in
Burgos, the other in Carrión;
this third I come to open today in Toledo
out of love for mio Cid, the man born in a good hour, that he
receive satisfaction from the heirs of Carrión, who, as we all know,
have wronged him gravely. Now,
let the judges of this matter be
counts don Enrique and don Ramón, and
these other counts who are not in the Carrión faction.
> You who are learned in law, be
> attentive and consider carefully,
> find out what is just, for I
> would command no injustice.
> > To one party and the other, I say,
> > that today we are at peace. If

anybody makes trouble in my court, I swear by Sant Isidro, he'll
lose my favor and be banished from the kingdom.
I'm on whichever side the justice is. And now,
let the Cid Campeador present his claim;
                    then we'll find out what
                the infantes of Carrión
            have to say."
        The Cid knelt to kiss the king's hands, then stood up:
        "My king and lord, I'm deeply grateful
        that you've held this court for my sake.
        This is my claim against the infantes de Carrión:
        that they abandoned my daughters does not dishonor me, O King,
        for it was you that married them. Today, you'll
        know what you have to do; but
when they carried my daughters away from the great city of Valencia,
I loved them sincerely, and showed it. I gave them the swords, Colada
and Tizón—and these I had won like a man—
so that they might do themselves honor, and
do you good service.
                When they left my daughters in the oak forest at Corpes, they
                showed there was nothing they wanted from me, and so
                        lost my love; they are
                        no longer my sons-in-law, let them
                            return me the swords."
The judges agreed, "This is all quite reasonable."
Said the count don García, "We'll answer this in a moment."
The infantes de Carrión and all their relatives
            went to one side, with the rest of their party,
                to discuss the question hurriedly, and to
                    formulate a reply.
"The Cid Campeador is even doing us a favor," they said, "not
bringing us to account today for dishonoring his daughters. That,
we ought to be able to square with King Alfonso. We'll
give him back the swords and that'll meet his claim;

when he has them back the court will break up, and
el Cid Campeador can make no further demands against us."
            This decided, they returned to the court.
                    "Grace, King Alfonso, O our lord!
                    We cannot deny it, he gave us two swords.
                    Since he demands their return and wants them back,
                    we wish herewith to return them.
                    You are our witness."
They brought out the swords, Colada and Tizón, and
put them in their lord's hands; the
swords are drawn and gleam throughout the hall, their
pommels and guards are pure gold;
the good men of the Court stand
                        wondering to see them.
The king called the Cid and gave him the swords. Taking them,
he kissed his hands and returned to the bench from which he came.
He held the swords in his hands and examined them closely;
they couldn't have pulled a switch on him—the Cid knew them too well.
He felt a joy rise through his body, and he smiled cheerfully,
raised his hand and stroked his beard:
            "By this beard of mine, which no man has ever pulled,
                now we'll proceed to the vengeance of doña Elvira
                    and doña Sol."
Calling his nephew don Pedro by name, he stretched out his arm
and gave him the sword of Tizón:
            Nephew, take it, it's found a better master."
Then, to Martín Antolínez, that worthy man of Burgos, he
        stretched out his arm and gave him the sword Colada:
            "Martín Antolínez, my worthy vassal, take
            Colada—I won it from a good master—
            Ramón Berenguer, count of Barcelona, that great town,
            I give it to you for that reason, take good care of it, I
            know that if the occasion presents itself, and it will,
            you'll win valor and renown."

Antolínez kissed his hand, received the sword.
      Then mio Cid Campeador arose once more:
      "Thanks be to the Creator and to you, my lord and king,
I'm satisfied in the matter of the swords,
      Colada and Tizón.
Now I've got another grievance against the heirs of Carrión.
When they took my daughters from Valencia, I gave them
three thousand marks
gold and silver:
that was what I did.
You know what they did to me, they gave me the business. Now
they're no longer my sons-in-law, let them return it."
Then you would have seen the infantes de Carrión really start whining!
Count don Ramón broke in:
      "Just tell him 'yes' or 'no.'
      The infantes replied:
      "Well, that's why we
      gave the Cid Campeador back his swords, that he
      should make no more demands on us, and the business finished."
Then count Ramón answered them:
"With the king's approval, we
decree as follows: you shall
comply with the Cid's demands."
The good king spoke and said, "I approve the judgment."
El Cid Campeador rose to his feet: "Look, either give me back
the money I've given you, or show reason for keeping it."
Then the infantes de Carrión walked to one side and consulted
but could come to no agreement, for the amount involved was enormous, and
      besides, they'd spent it already. They
      returned to the hall and gave the results
      of their discussion:
"The victor of Valencia presses this claim on us because he
covets our fortune so much. very well, we
agree to pay him out of income from

our lands in Carrión."
> When they had made this admission that
> they did owe the debt,
> the judges said:

"If this please the Cid, we shall not rule against it, but
in our own judgment, and we so decree, you
shall repay the monies here in court."
At these words, King Alfonso spoke:
> "We see clearly that in this suit, the
> Cid Campeador is only asking his rights.
> Between them, the infantes made me a gift,
> so I have two hundred of those three thousand marks. I
> should like to return it to them, that they pay it to the Cid.

I don't want any part of a dowry which they are obliged to return."
> Fernando González spoke, now, listen to this:
> "We do not have any available cash."

Count don Ramón answered him:
"So you've spent the silver and gold.
Our decree, then, in the presence of King Alfonso, is:
they shall pay in kind, and the Campeador
accept such payment."
The infantes de Carrión see
that there's nothing left to do.
> You'd have seen them lead in so many swift chargers,
> so many sturdy mules and well-broken palfreys, and
> so many fine swords and all sorts of armor.
> Mio Cid accepted it all
> at the court's appraisal value.

Besides the two hundred marks of theirs which King Alfonso had, the
infantes paid the Campeador what they could borrow elsewhere,
—their own goods were not enough.

So the infantes got out of the business badly,
and were mocked, now isn't that tough?

138   HIS CIVIL CLAIM FINISHED, THE CID PROPOSES A
CHALLENGE.

The Cid has taken the assessed goods,
given them to his men to look after.
This done, there still remained
        something to do:
          "Your grace, ya King my lord, for the love of charity!
          I cannot forget the larger grievance. Let
             all the court hear me
               and share my humiliation.
          The infantes de Carrión have dishonored me so basely, I
          can't let them off with anything less than a challenge.

139   HE ACCUSES THE INFANTES OF INFAMY.

          "Tell me, infantes of Carrión, have I done you any wrong?
          In jest, or in earnest, or in any fashion? If so,
          I'll set it right as this court decide.
          Why did you tear out my heartstrings?
          When you left Valencia I gave you my daughters
          along with high honor and abundant riches. If,
          you traitorous dogs, you did not love the girls, why
          did you take them and their honors from Valencia?
          Why did you attack them with cinches and your spurs?
          You left them deserted in the oak wood at Corpes,
          food for the wild beasts and mountain birds.
          For what you have done to them, I

denounce you as vile beyond villainy.[8]
If you give me no satisfaction,
let the court judge."

140   Contention between García Ordóñez and the Cid.

Then the count don García jumped to his feet:
"Ya, your mercy, King, greatest of all in Spain!
The Cid is clearly an old hand at answering summonses;
he lets his beard grow and wears it long
to make some men timid, others terrified.
The infantes de Carrión are of such high birth that they
ought not to want his daughters even for whores, and who
would imagine them as wives and equals? They
were quite right to leave them. Let the Cid talk,
we don't give a damn what he says."
Then the Campeador put his hand up to his beard:
"Praises be to God who commands heaven and earth, of course
my beard is long, it took its own time growing pleasantly.
What have you got going, count, to drag in my beard?
Since it started to grow it's taken its own sweet time, and
no son of woman has ever laid a hand on it, no one's ever
dared pull it, Moor or Christian, as
I pulled yours, Count, at the fortress at Cabra.
When I took Cabra, I seized you by the beard,
and there wasn't a kid there who didn't get his fistful.
And the hunk I tore out hasn't grown back yet, see?
Here it is.
I've carried it in my purse ever since!"

141   Fernando denies the accusation of villainy.

Fernando Gonzáles stood up and addressed the assembly loudly:

"We've had enough of your demands, Cid, leave off;
your goods have been returned to you, let this
suit between us go no further. We are
descended from the counts of Carrión, we
should marry daughters of emperors or kings, not
the daughters of some petty nobleman.
In leaving them, we did only what was right.
Because of it our worth is greater, not less,
and we'd have you know it."

142   THE CID AROUSES PEDRO BERMÚDEZ TO MAKE A
CHALLENGE.

Mio Cid Ruy Díaz fixed his gaze on Pedro Bermúdez:
"Speak up, Pedro, old dummy, you keep your mouth shut so tight.
All right, they're my daughters, but they're your first cousins, too;
the infantes are telling me off, but they bang your ears as well.
And if I answer the challenge, you know what chance you'll get to fight."

143   PEDRO BERMÚDEZ CHALLENGES FERNANDO.

Pedro Bermúdez began to speak,
stuttering, his tongue halted, he cannot break into words, but
once started, you know, he gives his tongue no rest:
"That's your way, Cid, you're always calling me
Pedro the Mute, and in court, too. You know
very well I can't do better, but when it
comes to action, you do not find me lacking.
Fernando,
every word you've said is a lie.
With the Campeador, you've received nothing but honor.
Now shall I tell you about your ways and means? Remember
when we were fighting near Valencia? You asked the loyal
Campeador for the honor of the first blows, saw a Moor and started to attack?

But before you got up to where he was, you turned tail.
If I hadn't arrived, that Moor
                    would have made a fair game of you.
            I galloped past you and engaged the Moor myself, it was
        I, not you, who struck the first blows and took him. I
gave you his horse and kept the whole thing secret.
Until today, I have spoken of it to no one. Then
        you boasted to the Cid and everyone else there that
            you'd killed the Moor, made yourself out a hero.
                Everyone believed you, but they didn't know the truth.
O, you're handsome enough to make a pretty bad coward! You
        tongue without hands, how is it you're bold enough to
                    open your mouth at all?

144   PEDRO BERMÚDEZ' CHALLENGE CONTINUES FOR A
WHILE.

        "So talk, Fernando, admit the truth of this,
            aren't you remembering that time in Valencia when
                the Cid was sleeping and the lion got loose?
And what you did, Fernando, in your funk? You crawled
under the bench of mio Cid Campeador!
That's where you hid, Fernando, and why I put you down today.
All of us stood around the bench to protect our lord until
he woke up, the man who had taken Valencia; and he
rose from the bench, walked toward the lion; the lion
waited for mio Cid with lowered head, and let himself
be taken by the mane and led back to his cage.
When he came back, the Cid saw all his vassals standing around,
he asked for his sons-in-law, no one could find them anywhere!
I challenge your body as villainous and a traitor, and
for the sake of the Cid's daughters, doña Elvira and doña Sol,

I'll do combat here in the presence of King Alfonso.
Leaving them like that, I say you're worth less than anything, I
could wipe you off with my finger. They're women and you're men
and in every way they're worthier than you. If it
please the Creator, when this combat's over, you
will spit it out, say with your own mouth that you're a traitor,
and whatever I've said here, you'll confess it to be truth."
    And here, between these two, talk ended.

145   DIEGO DENIES THE ACCUSATION OF INFAMY.

    Then Diego González spoke up.
      Listen to this:
"We are by birth from the purest lineage of counts.
O, that these marriages had never been entered into, whereby
we incurred family ties with mio Cid don Rodrigo!
We have never repented abandoning his daughters, let them
sigh for as long as they live, they
'll be mocked for the rest of their lives for what we did to them.
This I will uphold in combat against the hottest foe,
we did ourselves an honor, leaving them so."

146   MARTÍN ANDOLÍNEZ CHALLENGES DIEGO GONZÁLEZ.

    Martín Antolínez stood up and said:
"All right, you perfidious bastard, shut your lying mouth!
Did you forget the lion business too? You
        shot out the door into the courtyard
          and hid yourself behind the winepress beam; and I've
        not seen you wearing that shirt or cloak since.
That I'll maintain in combat with you, and I'll go the limit.
Because you left the Cid's daughters that way, I say

there is no way they are not better than you, and when
this fight is done, you'll say with your own mouth that
you're both a traitor and liar."

147   ASUR GONZÁLEZ ENTERS THE COURT.

These two, then, had finished with argument.
Asur González walked into the palace in an ermine cloak and his tunic trailing,
his face flushed, for he'd just finished eating.
What he had to say made little sense:

148   ASUR INSULTS THE CID.

"Ya, gentlemen, who's ever seen such crap as this?
Since when are we taking our honors from mio Cid de Bivar?
He ought to go back to the Ubierna River and hack away at his mills,
and charge his percentage of grain, like he's used to!⁹
Who'd ever think of marrying people like that to Carrión?"

149   MUÑO GUSTIOZ CHALLENGES ASUR GONZÁLEZ. MES-
SENGERS FROM NAVARRE AND ARAGÓN ASK THE CID FOR HIS
DAUGHTERS FOR THEIR KING'S SONS. ALFONSO CONSENTS TO THE
NEW MARRIAGES. MINAYA CHALLENGES THE INFANTES DE CAR-
RIÓN. GOMEZ PELÁEZ ACCEPTS THE CHALLENGE, BUT THE KING
FIXES THE TIME AND PLACE ONLY FOR THOSE CHALLENGES
WHICH ARE ALREADY ON THE BOOKS. THE KING WILL PROTECT
THE CID'S CHAMPIONS. THE CID OFFERS GIFTS TO EVERYONE WHO
IS LEAVING. (LACUNA: PROSE VERSION FROM THE CHRONICLE OF
TWENTY KINGS.) THE KING RIDES OUT OF TOLEDO WITH THE
CID. HE ORDERS THE CID TO RACE HIS HORSE.

Then Muño Gustioz got to his feet:
"Why don't you shut your filthy, traitorous mouth?
You fill your belly before you say your prayers in the morning,

and those you kiss at benediction have to smell your belches.
You've never spoken a word of truth
to friend or lord,
you're false to everyone, to God most of all.
I want no part of your sort of friendship, and
I'll make you admit you're everything I've said about you."
"Enough of these charges," Alfonso said;
"those who have already challenged will fight,
and that's the end. God help me."
And thus they closed the case.
At this point, two knights came into the court, one
called Ojarra, and the other Íñigo Jiménez: the
first was the petitioner for the prince of Navarre,
the other emissary of the infante de Aragón.
They kissed the hands of the king
don Alfonso, and
asked for the daughters of mio Cid
el Campeador, to be
future queens of Aragón and Navarre,
honored wives to those princes, and with all blessings.
At this, the court hushed and listened attentively.
Mio Cid el Campeador got to his feet:
"Your grace, my lord,
I give thanks to God
for this petition from Aragón and Navarre.
The last time,
it was you who married my daughters, and not I.
So here they are again in your hands.
I shall do nothing
without your express command."
The king rose and ordered silence in the court:
"You are sum and total, Cid Campeador.
Such a match will increase you in fiefs, estates, and honor.
I pray you, be satisfied with it,

then only shall I consent to it.
The arrangements for it will be made today in this court."
Rising, the Cid kissed the king's hands:
"When it pleases you, my lord, I give my consent."
Then the king said,
"God reward you well! Now, you,
Ojarra, and you, Íñigo Jiménez,
I hereby authorize this marriage,
the daughters of mio Cid, doña Elvira and doña Sol,
with the princes of Navarre and Aragón;
he may hand them over to you as their legal and blessed wives."
Ojarra and Íñigo Jiménez rose and kissed the king's hands, and then
those of mio Cid el Campeador.
They swore the oaths and gave their pledges that
it should be as had been said, or better. It
pleased everyone in the court greatly,
except, of course, the infantes de Carrión.
Minaya Álvar Fáñez then, stood up:
"Your permission, my lord and king, and
may it not displease the Cid Campeador, I've heard everyone today
have his say in court, and now
would like to say a few words of my own."
"Granted, with all my heart," said Alfonso.
"Speak, Minaya, say whatever you like."
"I ask you, and all the court, to hear what I have to say. I really have
something to face down with these infantes de Carrión.
Through King Alfonso's hand, it was I who gave them my cousins,
and they took them in marriage, all legally and blessed.
Mio Cid Campeador gave them vast wealth;
then they abandoned the girls, much to everyone's disgust.
I challenge their persons as monstrous traitors. You
are of the Beni-Gómez family, from which have come
worthy and valiant counts. Now we know better what
their tendencies are these days.

For this reason I thank God
      that the infantes of Navarre
        and Aragón have
asked for my cousins, doña Elvira and doña Sol; they
      used to be your equals and you
        held them in your arms;
          now, you will kiss their hands and
            call them 'my Lady' and humbly
acknowledge yourselves their servants, and that ought to get to you.
Thanks be to God, and to that king Alfonso that
      the honors still accrue
        to mio Cid el Campeador!
And you are, infantes, in every way, what I say you are,
and if anyone wants to answer me, say either yes or no, for I
      am Álvar Fáñez, a better man than any of you."
         Gómez Peláez then rose and said:
"All this talk, Minaya, tell me, what's the good of it?
There are many in this court brave enough to take you up on it,
and whoever would like to say otherwise, well, I'm here, and that's
his tough luck. God willing, we shall
come out of this, colors flying, and you'll
see later whether you're speaking truth or not."
        The king spoke: "All right, stop the wrangling now,
        let no man add another word to the argument.
The three against three, who challenged here in court,
will hold their combat
tomorrow morning at sunrise."
But then the infantes de Carrión spoke up again: "We cannot
         make it tomorrow, O King, give us a space of time. Our
         horses and arms, we gave them to the Campeador, so now
         we first have to go back to our lands in Carrión."
         The king spoke, handing it to the Campeador:
"This combat
shall be held where you command it."

The Cid replied, "I
shall not do it, my lord.
Much rather go back to Vaiencia alone
than go to Carrión."
Then the king said:
"That's all right, Campeador, give me
your knights and all their equipment,
they'll come with me,
I'll stand surety for them
as a lord should for any good vassal.
I'll see they're all right, and no count
or other nobleman shall do them harm.
Here in my court I set the time and place: the
combats will be fought on the meadows of Carrión
three weeks from today, and in my presence;
if anyone fail to appear,
he is forfeit, loses his point,
will be declared beaten, and
be shown a traitor."
The infantes de Carrión had no choice
but to accept his decision. Mio
Cid kissed the king's hands: "In your hands then, are my three knights.
I entrust them to you as
my king and lord.
They are entirely capable of fulfilling their trust.
Send them back to me in Valencia, with
the honors won, please God."
The king answered, "God grant it be so!"
The Cid Campeador threw back his hood,
took off his cap, white as the sun, undid the
cord and loosed his beard.
No one in the court could keep from staring at him. He
went over to the counts don Enrique and don Ramón and
hugged them also, begged them from his heart to take
whatever of his they liked.

To the others who'd been on his side, he
begged them also to choose from whatever he owned, what
            ever was to their liking; there were
some who did, and others who did not.
The two hundred marks, he told the king to
keep them, and take whatever else happened to please him.
        "God's love, I beg you mercy, King, now
            the business is settled, let me kiss your
                hands, have your blessing,
                    and let me be off to Valencia, you know
                        what it cost me to take it."
[Then the Campeador commanded that
the emissaries of Aragón and Navarre
            be given pack animals
            and everything else they needed, and
                sent on their way. Then,
with the highest men in his court, king don Alfonso saddled up to
ride out for a way with the Cid who was leaving the city.
And when they came to the Zocodover,[10] the king
said to the Cid who was riding along on his horse, Babieca:
"Don Rodrigo, you owe it to me to race that horse of yours now, of which
    I've heard such good things said."
        The Cid began to smile, and answered:
            "My lord, there are many nobles and seasoned men
                here in your court, happy to follow your bidding.
                    Have them put their mounts through the paces."
                The king replied:
"I am pleased with your answer, but nonetheless,
I want you to run that horse,
                    to please me, all right?"

150   THE KING ADMIRES BABIECA, BUT WILL NOT ACCEPT
HIM AS A GIFT. THE CID'S FINAL ORDERS TO HIS THREE FIGHTERS.
THE CID RETURNS TO VALENCIA. THE KING AT CARRIÓN. THE DAY
OF COMBAT ARRIVES. THE HEIRS TRY TO HAVE COLADA AND

TIZÓN BARRED FROM THE COMBAT. THE CID'S MEN ASK THE KING
FOR HIS PROTECTION, AND RIDE OUT ONTO THE FIELD OF BATTLE.
THE KING DESIGNATES THE FIELD JUDGES, AND ADMONISHES THE
INFANTES. THE JUDGES MAKE THEIR PREPARATIONS FOR THE
FIGHT. THE FIRST CLASH. PEDRO BERMÚDEZ DEFEATS FERNANDO.

The Cid, then, set spur to the horse
who raced off in such a blaze of speed
that everyone who was there was thunderstruck.]
The king raised his hand and made the sign of the cross: "I swear,
by Sant Isidro of León, there is no
better man than that in all our realm."
Mio Cid rode up and stopped the horse before him, to
kiss the hand of his lord, Alfonso:
"You bid me race Babieca, my swift horse, there's
not another like him in any land, Moor or Christian,
not today, there isn't.
I give him to you as a gift. Take him, my lord."
The king said, "I'd rather not, if I took that horse from you,
it is sure he would not have so good a master.
A horse like this needs a rider like you
to defeat Moors in the field and pursue them after.
Anyone who tries to take him from you, God's curse on him.
You and your horse have brought honor to our throne."
They took their leave then,
and the court turned back.
The Campeador laid it out also
to his men,
who had the fighting to do:
"Ya, Martín Antolínez, and you Pedro Bermúdez,
and Muño Gustioz, my worthy vassal,
you've got to conduct yourselves like men in the field.
I want you to send good news back to me in Valencia."
Martín Antolínez said, "No call to say that, my lord!

We've taken the debt on ourselves,
    and it's we shall pay it out. You might have
       word of dead men, but of vanquished ones?
       No."
The man born in a good hour was pleased at this response, and
took leave of them, his friends, and they were his friends.
The Cid headed toward Valencia, and the king toward Carrión.
    But the three weeks stipulated are now ended.
    The
       Campeador's men are at the appointed place, wanting
to accomplish the obligations laid upon them by their lord. They
       are under the protection of Alfonso de León.
They spend two days waiting for the infantes de Carrión.
Well, they came, very well set up with their horses and equipment and
all their relatives as well, and it was agreed
that if they could isolate the Cid's men, they
       would fall on them in the field and kill them
       to the dishonor of their lord.
So their intentions were very evil, but
the plot didn't get off the ground, so
great was their fear of Alfonso de León.
       The Cid's champions sit vigil by their arms, the
       night's cut into pieces and the day comes. Many
       rich men have gathered at the site to see
       a fight that will give them pleasure and
furthermore and above all else, of course, King don Alfonso to
see justice done, and no treachery be permitted. Not to anyone.
       The Campeador's men have already armored up,
       and since they serve one lord, are taking
       counsel together to agree on strategy.
Elsewhere, the infantes de Carrión are arming and
being advised by count García Ordóñez.
They petitioned the king to bar
Colada and Tizón from the combat,

that the Campeador's men not use them—
the infantes regretted deeply having returned them. They
laid it before the king, but he would not condone it.
    "You raised no objection when arrangements were made at the court.
        If your swords are good, they will serve you well,
            as will those of the Campeador's men serve them.
Now get up, infantes de Carrión, get out on the field,
    what you have to do now is fight like men;
        I do not think the Cid's men will lack for anything.
If you carry the field, you will have won great honor,
    and if you're defeated, don't blame us, for
        everyone knows you brought this on yourselves."
Now the infantes de Carrión are really repentant,
regret deeply the things they've done, and would
not have done them now for everything in Carrión.
    King Alfonso goes to inspect the Cid's champions;
    all three are armored up and speak to the king:
        "We kiss your hands, as our king and lord;
        be a faithful judge today between them and us,
        help us to justify the right and permit no foul play.
The infantes have a whole slew of relatives with them, and we
can't tell whether or not they're planning treachery.
Our lord, the Cid, has placed us in your hands,
for the love of heaven, see that we get our rights!"
    Then the king said, "With all my heart!"
        They lead good, fast horses out to them.
        The Cid's men bless the saddles
          and mount with celerity.
Shields with heavy bosses hang from their necks and
into their hands they take the spears with sharp iron tips;
each of the lances has a pennon.
With many good men all around them, they rode out to the
    field where the lists were marked off. The
        Campeador's men are all three in agreement,

each will attack his foe forcibly.
There at the other end
are the infantes de Carrión,
well attended, since they have
so many relatives.
The king appoints judges to pronounce what is right and what not,
and no one is to argue with their "yes" or their "no."
When everything was set on the field, King
Alfonso addressed them:
"Now hear what I'm saying, infantes de Carrión:
this fight should have come off in Toledo, but
you wanted it otherwise.
These three champions of mio Cid Campeador
I have brought to the lands of Carrión under my personal guarantee of safety.
Now, defend your cause and no dirty fighting. If anyone
wants to try any tricks, I am here to prevent it, and
he will not find himself welcome anywhere in my kingdom."
This announcement depresses the infantes even more.
The judges and the king pointed out the boundary markers, and cleared
everyone standing around from off the field.
The six combatants are informed clearly
that anyone who moves beyond the boundaries will
be declared vanquished.
The spectators draw back on all sides of the field
and are to stay six spear-lengths
away from the boundary lines.
They drew lots for the ends of the field,
which were arranged so that no one had to face into the sun;
the judges leave the center of the field.
They are face to face,
the Cid's men in position
against those of Carrión,
and the infantes facing the men of the Campeador, each one
his attention fixed on his opponent.

They hold their shields over their heart-side and lower
    the pennant-flying lances, and
        bending low over the saddletrees,
            strike spurs to horses, the earth
                thundered where they ran. Each
man kept his eyes on his opponent, three against three they clash together,
everyone who's watching them expects them all to be knocked off dead.
        Pedro Bermúdez, who had been the first to challenge,
        came face to face with Fernando González, each
        fearlessly aims a blow at the other's shield.
Fernando González' lance struck through don Pedro's shield
but drives upon empty space, misses the target of flesh, and
the lance snaps in two places.
Pedro Bermúdez does not fall from this, but sits firm in the saddle,
and for that blow he has taken, strikes one of his own that
splits the center boss of the opposing shield and throws it flying,
smashed straight through, nothing withstands him, the spear
        drives into the chest near the heart.
           Fernando was
wearing three thicknesses of chain mail, which saved him.
The first two folds gave way, but the third held, but
      the shirt, the tunic, and this third layer of mail were
        driven a hand's breadth into the flesh and
          blood spouted from his mouth.
Fernando's cinches snapped,
not one of them held firm, and he
tumbles ass over backward off the horse. It
appeared to the people there, the wound so bad it must have killed him.
Bermúdez drops the lance and draws his sword. As soon
as Fernando González sees that, he recognizes Tizón, and
before the stroke can fall, he cries,
          "I'm beaten!"

The judges pronounce the defeat
verified.
And Pedro Bermúdez walked off and left him.

151   MARTÍN ANTOLÍNEZ DEFEATS DIEGO.

Don Martín and Diego González charged each other so furiously
and the blows struck were so powerful that both lances were shattered.
Martín Antolínez drew the sword, which shone so bright and clear,
            its blade illumined the whole field;
                it struck a blow which caught
                    Diego from the side,
                        split off the covering helmet,
sheared through the holding thongs, tore off the hood of mail, and came
to the cloth cap underneath, cut through both cap and head mail, sheared
the hair from the head and came to flesh, the upper
part of the head armor fell off, clanked on the ground, the lower
half held.
            When the mighty Colada had struck this blow,
            Diego González saw he would not escape with his life.
            He reins his horse to face his opponent, he
            has a sword in his hand, but does not wield it.
Then Martín Antolínez meets him with sword again, gave him a blow
with the flat of the sword, not the cutting edge.
Then the infante begins to scream loudly, "O God of glory, help me,
Lord, save me from this sword!"
                    Reining back his horse and
                    keeping out of sword reach, he
                    edged him beyond the markers.
                Don Martín stood on the field.
            The king then calls to Martín Antolínez,
            "Come over here and keep me company;

with what you've done, you've won the battle."
The judges concur with the truth of the king's words.

152   MUÑO GUSTIOZ DEFEATS ASUR GONZÁLEZ. THE FATHER
OF THE INFANTES DECLARES THE CONTEST LOST. THE CID'S
CHAMPIONS RETURN CAREFULLY TO VALENCIA. THE CID'S JOY. HIS
DAUGHTERS ARE MARRIED FOR A SECOND TIME. THE JUGLAR
ENDS HIS POEM.

Those two have triumphed. Now I'll tell you of
Muño Gustioz, and how his fight
with Asur González went.
Great were the blows struck each against the other's shield; Asur
González was strong and valiant, ran
against the shield of Muño Gustioz,
drove through the shield, breached the armor, but the lance broke through onto
nothing, did not touch flesh.
This blow struck, Muño Gustioz struck another, which
shattered the shield at the center boss.
Nothing could stop the blow, it split the armor,
prised it apart, and though not near the heart, the lance—pennon and all—
ran through his body, came out on the other side a full arm's length. Then
Gustioz twisted the spear to one side and tumbled his foe from the saddle,
drew out the lance and threw him to earth. The head, pennon, and
shaft emerged dripping red. Everyone is sure the wound is mortal.
Muño Gustioz readies his dripping lance and stands
poised over the fallen man.
Gonzalo Ansúrez cries, "For God's sake,
don't strike him! The field is won, this thing is finished!"[11]
The judges said, "We heard that. Thank you."
The good King Alfonso commanded the field be cleared;
the arms of the losers left thereon he kept for himself.[12]
The Campeador's men departed with great honor,
having won the contest, thanks to the Creator.
People were downhearted

all over Carrión.
The king sent the Cid's men off by night so that
there would be less danger that somebody might jump them.
Taking their precautions, they
    travel day and night,
      until they come to Valencia
        and into the Cid's presence.
          They've left the heirs of Carrión proven blackguards,
          completed the task commanded by their lord.
          Can't tell you how pleased the Campeador was.
        And great is the humiliation of the infantes de Carrión.
        Whoever scorns a good lady and afterward deserts her, may he
      come to such a bad end, a worse one even!
So let us leave the heirs of Carrión to their troubles,
certainly, they've taken no pleasure from them.
Let us speak now of him who was born in a good hour.
        In Valencia the great, great are the celebrations,
        for the Cid's men have carried off the honor.
        Their lord, Ruy Díaz, tugged at his beard:
          "Thanks be to the King of heaven,
            my daughters are avenged.
        Now they are well quit of their estates in Carrión! No
      mortgages to pay! And now,
whomever it please or displease, I
shall marry them without shame."
        The infantes of Navarre and Aragón renew their suits, and
        all are met together with Alfonso de León. They
          solemnize the marriage of doña Elvira and doña Sol.[13]
The first weddings were grand, but these are spectacular, for he
marries them to greater honors than they had before.
        He who was born in a good hour,
        see how his honors increase, for now
          his daughters are queens
            of Aragón and Navarre.
Today, the kings of Spain are descended from him,[14]

and all honor reaches down from him, who was in good hour born.
Mio Cid, lord of Valencia,
passed from this world on
the day of Pentecost,
may Christ grant him pardon!
May He pardon us all, the
just and sinners alike!
These, then, were the deeds
of mio Cid el Campeador;
in this place
       the story's ended.

May he who wrote this book
have paradise of God.
Per Abbat wrote this down
the month of May 1345.[15]

The story's finished.[16]
If you do not have money,
give us wine.
Or throw us anything of value,
jewels, clothing, any-
thing will do instead.

Notes

The First Cantar. The Cid's Exile

1.   The gesture was no light impertinence: The Cid's own enormous beard is repeatedly mentioned as epithet later in the poem, a symbol of his manhood. To pull a man's beard was a profound insult. Oaths were sworn by a man's beard, and no one was to touch it.

2.   Kissing the hand or foot of the lord was clearly the mode of entering upon or renewing the pact of vassalage. It is the sign of submission, not necessarily one of affection.

3.   Emirs were Moorish military commanders. Valencia, and, indeed, half of Spain, was in Moorish hands at that time.

4.   The Moors used drums to create a thunderous roar before and during battles to unnerve their enemies. Those who heard the sound for the first time were terrified and thought it was an earthquake.

5.   El Poyo is a town located on the left bank of the Jiloca, on the road between Sagunto and Calatayud, dominated by that hill, which is 4,025 feet above sea level. El Poyo is about 6.2 miles from Monreal, 21.7 miles from Daroca, 31 miles from Molina and Cella, and 40.4 miles from Teruel, which should give an idea of the scope of the Cid's operation from there.

6.   A kingly joke: the taking and defense of Alcocer alone took eighteen weeks. So five or six months of exile have passed already at this point.

7.   Inaccurate prediction on the singer's part. The *de mio Cid* part of the name sank into those valleys and was lost.

8.   It was those low cantles on the Catalan horses. Always use a Galician saddle.

9.   Pun on the word *franco;* the Cid frees the count, who is a Frank.

THE SECOND CANTAR. THE WEDDING OF THE CID'S DAUGHTERS

1.   Jérica, Onda, Almenara, and Burriana are all towns in the southern part of Castellón, just north of the province of Valencia. But the poet is jamming history a bit here: the Cid stayed around Burriana until 1091, but did not seize Almenara until 1098, after the conquest of Valencia. The same applies to Murviedro, 18 miles north of Valencia: it was taken only in 1098, after Valencia had fallen to the Cid.

2.   Benicadell, or Peña Cadiella, is the range that separates the provinces of Valencia and Alicante. The Cid rebuilt the castle of Benicadell in the year 1092. It was a highly strategic location, controlling the roads from Valencia and Játiva to Alcoy and Alicante.

3.   After 1091, Sevilla, conquered by the Almorávides from North Africa, could not properly be said to have kings. But the Arabic equivalent had a great deal more spread, so that any Moorish emir or general was normally called "king," and the "king of Sevilla" referred to here is whatever North African general was then commanding Sevilla.

4.   Kissing the lord's hand was not only a symbol of vassalage, but also, apparently, required form for an honorable discharge. In taking off, the soldier or knight kissed his lord's hand and said: "I kiss your hand and take my leave of you, and from this time forward, I am no longer your vassal." We still use the term, "kissoff."

5.   Two young men who were more noble than wealthy. *Infante* was a term used either for the sons of kings or of others variously related. Three infantes de Carrión figure in the poem: Diego and Fernando, who were, according to the poem, eventually husbands of the Cid's daughters, and Asur, all three sons of Gonzalo Ansúrez and nephews of Pedro Ansúrez, count of Carrión.

6.   Though this is the last mention of Raquel and Vidas and the dubious business of the trunks, there is no reason to think that the Cid did not reward them with largesse.

7.   The Guardarrama range separates the drainage basin of the Tajo from that of the Duero.

8.   Documents refer to the Cid's daughters by their baptismal names, Cristina and María, not Elvira and Sol, which must have been for the use of family and the circle of acquaintances.

9.   *Rogadores* were formal go-betweens or petitioners who solemnly asked the father for the bride. The sense here seems best rendered by the verb "to second," since Alfonso is technically acting as petitioner here, not just as king, and asks the nobles present to join him in interceding for the infantes. You will see, in this cantar and the next, that the Cid avoids the direct responsibility for giving his daughters to the heirs by transferring their jurisdiction to Alfonso, granting him power to do as he thinks best in the matter.

10.   The exchange of swords was a formal ceremony establishing a family relationship. The importance of this will be seen in the Third Cantar, where the famous swords Colada and Tizón are given a primary import.

11.   As is still common in Mediterranean countries, the civil ceremony preceded the religious.

12.   This is a reference to King Alfonso. The reading is highly doubtful, because the manuscript is somewhat damaged at this place. In order to sustain the interest of his audience, the

singer, at this point, pretends not to know the fate that awaits the Cid's daughters, a ploy comparable to the close of a radio or television serial: "Will Elvira and Sol find happiness with the infantes, Fernando and Diego? Tune in tomorrow, to the third and final cantar of this series: *The Atrocity at Corpes!"*

THE THIRD CANTAR. THE ATROCITY AT CORPES

1.   According to the statutes of Leon and of Carrión, confirmed by Queen Urraca in 1109, a knight was exempted from going to war during the first year of his marriage. The Cid reminds them of their wives, although it's been two years since their marriage. In short, the Cid gives them an out, should they need it.

2.   The *amo* or *ayo* was the instructor who watched over a young man in his first trial of arms.

3.   Elpha is a lady unknown to history.

4.   Although the girls are mentioned as young for matrimony, this is only one of several references indicating that the marriages were fully consummated.

5.   Doña Urraca was the sister of Alfonso and the assassinated Sancho. It is said that she was Alfonso's mistress and had Sancho killed so as to leave Alfonso in a stronger position politically with León as well as Castille. Why is history or, in this case, pretty reliable gossip always more interesting than fiction? La Torre is some 4½ miles east of San Esteban.

6.   Note that earlier in this chapter, Diego Téllez is referred to as Álvar Fáñez's man. San Esteban is clearly a town that pays tribute to Minaya, hence the generous offerings when he arrives. The earlier gifts of grain, meat, and wine to Muñoz and the two girls upon their arrival in town, though they might be construed as duties to their lord's cousins, were probably more gifts of sympathy than anything else.

7.   *Vistas* and *juntas* were less solemn assemblies of judicial officers, usually district officers, than the *cortes*, more often presided over by the king. Much of the litigation was decided by decree, but often there was the spectacle of trial by combat, as we shall see.

8.   Challenge to combat could be given only for bodily harm, a slap in the face or pulling a man's beard, or for an offense against honor, not for reasons of material loss. *Menos valedes vos* (You are worth less [than I]) was an extremely serious insult.

9.   The Ubierna River runs near Bivar. *Maquilas* were the amounts of flour or grain paid to the miller as the price of grinding. Asur's taunt is not that the Cid owns mills; every great estate owned them and had some income from them, including Carrión and the king himself, according to Menéndez Pidal. Asur is insulting the Cid here by pretending that he took a direct part in the operation of the mills, like a small businessman instead of a great lord.

10.   *Zocodover*, an Arab word meaning a circular marketplace, is one of the two principal plazas in Toledo.

11.   With the shock of the blow and the graveness of the wound, Asur has clearly lost consciousness and cannot say "uncle," so rather than let Gustioz kill him, Gonzalo Ansúrez, historically his father and father of the infantes, concedes for him. Whoever is the one who gets clobbered in these judicial duels or combats must speak and admit that, not only is he beaten, but that the other guy was right to begin with. Otherwise, he accepts death, rather than back down.

12.   That is, he told his majordomo to go impound what was left. The king had the right to the horses and arms of traitors, i.e., whoever happened to lose these judicial combats. The same thing happened in the case of an exile.

13.   The second marriages are the historically recorded ones. Whatever the poet claims, the Cid's daughters did not become

queens of Navarre and Aragón. Cristina, the elder daughter, married Ramiro, lord of Monzón, an infante of Navarre. Their son, García Ramírez, ascended the throne of Navarre in 1134. María Rodriguez, the Cid's younger daughter, married Ramón Berenguer III, count of Barcelona and the nephew of Ramón II, the one defeated by the Cid early in the story. The simplification (or confusion) of the poet seems to result from the fact that Ramón Berenguer IV became prince of Aragón in 1137 by marrying the daughter of Ramiro the Monk. Catalunya and Aragón from that point became the kingdom of Aragón. But Ramón IV, though the son of Ramón III, was not María's child. From that marriage there were two daughters. One, named Jimena after her grandmother, married Roger III, count of Foix in the south of France.

14.   In 1140, to prevent a war between the king of Navarre, García Ramírez (grandson of the Cid), and Alfonso VII, emperor of Castille, a mediation committee of bishops and relatives of the principals arranged a marriage of their children: the Princess Blanca de Navarre, great-granddaughter of the Cid, with Sancho, the heir of Castille. The marriage was consummated in 1151, and their son, Alfonso VIII, was the first king of Castille descended from the Cid. His daughters carried the blood of Ruy Díaz to the royal house of Portugal in 1208 and to that of Aragón in 1221.

15.   This date is old-style; new-style, it would be A.D. 1307. Per Abbat is, of course, the copyist, not the poet.

16.   This juglar's note was added in the fifteenth century by another hand.

Selected References

Available Editions of the *Poem of the Cid* in Spanish

Poema de Mío Cid. 10th ed. Edited with Notes by Ramón Menéndez Pidal. Clásicos Castellanos. Madrid: Espasa-Calpe, 1963.

Poema de Mío Cid. 5th ed. Edited with Notes by Ian Michael. Clásicos Castalia. Madrid: Editorial Castalia, 1984.

Historical Studies and Background Material

Deyermond, Alan D. *Epic Poetry and the Clergy: Studies on the "Mocedades de Rodrigo."* London: Tamesis, 1969.

MacKay, Angus. *Spain in the Middle Ages: From Frontier to Empire, 1000–1500.* New York: St. Martin's Press, 1977.

Menéndez Pidal, Ramón. *En torno al Poema del Cid,* Barcelona: E.D.H.A.S.A., 1963.
———. *La España del Cid.* 2 vols. Madrid: Espasa-Calpe, 1956.
———. *Poesía juglaresca y orígenes de las literaturas románicas.* Madrid: Instituto de Estudios Políticos, 1957.
———. *Reliquias de la poesía épica española.* Madrid: Espasa-Calpe, 1951.

O'Callaghan, Joseph F. *A History of Medieval Spain.* Ithaca: Cornell University Press, 1975.